WOMAN – THE FAILED MALE

The Missing Link in Theories
of Male Superiority

Dr Geraldine Sharp

HONORA-PUBLISHING
BUMBLE BEE COTTAGE   NEW ROAD
CALLINGTON

ISBN 978-0-9955875-0-2
Printed in Great Britain by
Arthur H. Stockwell Ltd
Torrs Park   Ilfracombe
Devon EX34 8BA

CONTENTS

ACKNOWLEDGEMENTS

This book would not have been possible without the scholarship of Peter Brown, whose work first opened my eyes to the significance of semen, feminist scholarship on women's history, and women's place in Christian sexual theology.

Thanks go to my husband Sid, who has supported me both practically and emotionally over six years of research. My great appreciation also to Karen Dolman who provided detailed feedback as the book progressed.

I am particularly grateful to the following people, who gave generously of their time to read the penultimate draft and provide valuable impressions and comments: R. Campbell (Australia), S. Qoraishi (Qatar), J. Zhang (China), L. Dunn (USA), P. Began, G. Buttery and B. Mellor (UK).

DEDICATION

To my grandchildren and their generation

INTRODUCTION

This book is about semen; semen is the missing link in theories of male superiority. We are about to embark on a journey that peels away centuries of beliefs and 'truths' about women and about men. In the modern world, we still see men dominate in all spheres of influence. This is despite the acceptance by many nations of basic human rights as outlined in the International Convention on Human Rights following the Second World War; the advances in the education of women and girls; and the gradual collapse of some of the traditional ideas about women's innate inferiority in some parts of the world. Yet old ideas about women's characteristics and roles continue. Male-dominated societies and organisations tend to refer to 'tradition' and/or culture when defending the male 'right' to control, discipline and assign roles to women. But where did these traditions originate? Whose ideas were they? When did they begin? Why do they continue to persist? Do they stand up under scrutiny?

I had listened to the standard 'truths' for male superiority and found them wanting. For example, the claim that men are physically stronger than women – yes, men can have up to ten per cent more muscle strength than women; yet the majority of hard labour in the world is done by women. Surely, some of those women have more muscle strength than some men. More male than female babies tend to have congenital defects at birth; boys tend to have more childhood illnesses than girls; women live longer than men. So, how can all men be 'stronger' than all women in every respect? Some men and some women have similar physical strength; and some do not succumb to childhood illness regardless of their sex; and some men live longer than women. The statement 'Men are stronger than women' cannot be applied to all men and all women, therefore it is not a 'truth'.

Neither is the presumption that men are more intelligent than women. Some men are more intelligent than some women, but some women are more intelligent than some men. The truth is that some people are more intelligent than other people. A man's presumed greater intelligence is not a 'truth'. Men are presumed to be the 'warriors'; they protect women and children. Not true. Some men are warriors, but some women have also been warriors and continue to be so. Some children are also forced or encouraged to be warriors. Men are not the only warriors; and not all women need protecting. None of the 'truths' associated with male superiority explain why men believed, and continue to believe, themselves to be superior, because they can so easily be disproved. They certainly did not explain the presumption that *all* men were superior to *all* women. So, where did these notions come from? Who said what and why? This is the purpose of our expedition, to discover how these 'truths' came about.

Where do we start in this quest for origins? We could begin with the age of the Great Mother, from as late as 7000 BC, which proceeded the age of the male God. Women historians have comprehensively outlined the evidence for the reverence, respect and fear in which women were held in many societies. It is not necessary to repeat this scholarship here. In our search for the origins of traditions which have subordinated women we shall begin in the Mediterranean basin around 2,000 years ago. This is a good place to begin, not least because the ideas and beliefs of Ancient Greece, Judaism, Christianity and Imperial Rome formed the basis of later European thought. So, what were the beliefs, attitudes and practices accepted as 'natural' and God-given in the ancient world? Can we see traces of these ideas in contemporary society? Which traditional ideas about women and about men continue to exist? Which traditional beliefs, attitudes and practices are still considered valid in the twenty-first century? Has anything changed?

We need a clear pathway with staging posts if we are to follow the ideas and beliefs of the ancient world and religious thought. We shall follow the ideas of the Greek philosophers and physicians, the Hebrew Creation story and the development of Christian sexual theology. It is not the only approach we could take, but it provides a lens on ideas in the ancient world and religious thought that have provided legitimisation for the primary 'truth' for man's presumed superiority – the possession of semen.

The belief in man's superiority led to the subordination of women. Chapter One reminds us that at the root of the control of women and children is the institution of patriarchy, which often combines with a hatred of women. Patriarchy has been supported by tradition and legislation, which in turn was underpinned by religious beliefs and myths. Patriarchal hierarchies of power have been used to control lesser males, women and children. Patriarchs at the macro and micro levels of society have imposed their ideas and values on the rest of society. Patriarchy is an apparatus of power that defines men as superior to women.

Chapter Two begins our trail of semen down through the ages with an outline of the beliefs and 'truths' held by Greek philosophers and physicians who expressed contemporary ideas about the properties of semen. Semen was uniquely male. It was what made men 'men'. Nature intended all foetuses to be male. In Greek discourse, woman was a mistake of nature, a 'failed male'. The possession of semen and resulting fantasies provided a 'biological basis' for all the positive characteristics assigned to men; and led to the legitimisation of man's domination of women, children and the natural world. This semen mythology provided the foundation of man's presumed superiority and the later Christian elevation of semen to the 'divine' and the presumed access to 'truth' by a celibate male hierarchy.

We then consider the development of the early Christian Church, which originated in the Mediterranean basin influenced by Hebrew beliefs and practices, and 'common sense' notions about male superiority that arose from Greek ideas about the role and qualities of semen. In Greek philosophy, a mythology of semen supported and sustained a patriarchal ideology. The Hebrew story of Creation, together with this mythology of semen, was fundamental to patriarchal beliefs and organisation, and to an emerging Christian sexual theology. The Creation story ensured that woman was to blame for the entry of sin into the world and later provided justification for the Christian theologian Augustine's belief in 'original sin'.

Sexual stereotypes are examined in Chapter Four. Semen mythology led to a discourse which justified the assignment of all positive characteristics to men and consigned to woman the polar opposites. Men 'naturally' assigned to themselves all positions of power in society; women were in need of guidance and control due to their physical and mental weakness. Woman's main role was to service a man materially and sexually, bear a man's child and care for the sick. Man lived in fear of a descent into the undifferentiated state of a woman and was concerned to exclude all signs of 'softness', which might suggest a loss of manhood. There is evidence that for a man to be a man, a sufficient supply of semen was vital. He had to strive to remain virile; semen must therefore be protected. As we shall see in later chapters these Greek and Hebrew stereotypes of masculinity and femininity have stood the test of time.

The phallus became the symbol of male power. Through the possession of semen and its organ of transmission, man appropriated the primary role in reproduction; in so doing, he elevated himself almost to the divine. His sacred organ of generation, the phallus, was the source of all human life. Man adopted the status of 'co-creator' with God. Women's organs and emissions were an abomination. Fear of women and of the power of sexuality, prejudice and notions of uncleanness associated with menstrual blood and childbirth all contributed to negative beliefs about women in the world from which the second Abrahamic religion – Christianity – sprang. When, in the third century, orthodox Christianity became the established religion of Imperial Rome, patriarchy as an apparatus of power supported both religion and politics. A monotheistic patriarchal religion swept across Europe together with the Imperial Roman armies; and the state gradually became the guarantor of patriarchal power. Biblical scholarship has shown that women played a full part in the development of both the orthodox and Gnostic Churches. However, in the orthodox Church women were gradually excluded from participation in worship or prophecy. By the end of the second century, women's participation in worship was explicitly condemned. All traces of women's participation in the life and work of the orthodox Church were erased.

One of the most significant stages on our journey, which provided the foundations of Christian sexual theology, is what three theologians – Augustine (354 – 430), Albert (c.1200 – 1280) and Aquinas (1225 – 1274) – said about women and sexuality. Augustine's doctrine of 'original sin' confirms woman as the site and cause of sin in the world. Albert exhibits a hatred of women in his slanderous writings. He also said that when a woman says no to sexual activity she really means yes. In the Middle Ages, Aquinas, the pupil of Albert, elevates semen to the 'divine'; uses the recently rediscovered ancient Greek texts to 'prove' patriarchal beliefs about women and affirms women's role as the incubator for man's 'seed'. He could see no other possible use woman could be.

The institution of celibacy is significant because it elevated the male celibate almost to the 'divine'. Celibacy became a requirement for all who held power in the Christian Church, and a male, celibate hierarchy imposed its beliefs on the rest of the clergy and the people. We shall see that the requirement of continence (sexual renunciation) has not always been linked to priesthood; nor has continence and priesthood been a constant tradition in the Christian Churches. Nevertheless, eventually the male continent body was afforded privileged access to 'truth'. It is the retention of semen which supports the power of the clerical caste in the orthodox Christian Church. The institution of celibacy is an apparatus of male power, which reinforces traditional ideas about men and women and is the backbone of the patriarchal, orthodox Catholic Church.

The Scientific Revolution, the Renaissance and the Reformation resulted in a new world view. In Chapter Nine we note the impact of the Reformation – not least, the notion of individual access to truth and to God which emerged. This was the greatest challenge to the power of the priesthood. The Christian Church split into two main groups, the orthodox and the Protestants. The Catholic Christian Church reaffirmed orthodox 'truths' as absolute, and reacted to the 'errors of modernism' by retrenchment. The Catholic Christian Church became a fortress. There was no Reformation for semen or for women.

The Second Vatican Council (1962–65) was heralded as the 'New Epiphany' for the Catholic Church; but there was no epiphany for semen or for women. In the encyclical *Humanae Vitae* (1968), protection of semen continued as the imperative to forbid the use of the contraceptive pill. The ban led to the maturation of individual conscience among many Catholics, as they resisted the ban. The authority of the Pope and priests declined following the encyclical; and the power of the clergy to control the sexual lives of women and men was severely diminished. In the Western world, confession went into decline and with it one of the most powerful tools with which to control the laity disappeared.

Does patriarchy continue to exist in the twenty-first century? Do patriarchal ideas about women continue to exist and have meaning? Do traditional ideas continue to define women and their role? In modern-day patriarchy, some women have experienced some mitigation of the worst effects of patriarchy, particularly in the Western world; but generally, women are still striving to achieve equality with men. The evidence is that progress towards equality in many parts of the world has stopped, even if it had ever begun. A new era of patriarchy has emerged in which violence has proliferated; self-hatred has flourished, violence against women, especially rape, is committed daily with impunity and sex trafficking thrives. The oppression of women will continue in many parts of the world as 'cultural and traditional', unless the foundation of a presumed superiority (semen) is recognised for the nonsense that it is. The world religions have a significant role to play if equality is to be achieved. Religion plays an important role in culture and tradition. Secular organisations such as the United Nations can only achieve so much if religious traditions continue to uphold the presumption of male superiority. Once the root of this presumption is exposed as nonsense, religious leaders have a moral duty to revise their doctrines.

CHAPTER ONE:

PATRIARCHY: MEN ARE SUPREME

Before we begin on our journey to follow the trail of semen down through the ages, we shall briefly look at what is meant by patriarchy. The institution of patriarchy is evident in many societies and religions and is often combined with misogyny. Patriarchy in the family and in the wider society has been supported by tradition and legislation, which in turn has been underpinned by religious beliefs and myths. Patriarchy is evident not only in the world's three main Abrahamic religions of Judaism, Christianity and Islam, but also in almost all other forms of religious and secular organisations. Religious and secular ideas are often mutually supportive. Patriarchy is based on a presumption of male superiority; therefore, it is necessary to consider how secular ideas and religious myths and doctrines have supported this notion. We shall also see if and how these notions have continued down through the ages, or if they have changed in light of advances in science and new thinking.

Patriarchy is a universal scheme for domination by birthright; merely to be born male is sufficient to claim superiority over women.[1] Why should this be sufficient? What ideas and beliefs underpin this assumption? In order to answer these questions we have to unpick some of the most basic beliefs about what it is to be 'man' and what it is to be 'woman' in any particular society. Certain characteristics are expected or presumed of men and women, which roles they will undertake in society, and the status of each sex in society. Women and men are expected to fulfil roles considered 'natural' and 'normal'. In order that men and women keep to their assigned roles, there must be consent. Consent is achieved through the socialisation of both sexes at family and societal levels. Socialisation begins in infancy, in the family. It is here that the norms of a particular society begin to be absorbed. Later, schooling, peer pressure and/or societal expectations combine to obtain consent to society's norms in relation to what it means to be a man or a woman. In many societies, male superiority has been accepted as 'natural', 'normal' or 'traditional', yet different types of social arrangements over a range of societies suggest that few roles are 'natural' or 'normal'. For example, in some societies it is considered normal for women and children to perform hard labour. In others, it is normal for men to fulfil this role. In some societies only men hold positions of power, while in others women share power with men. Societal roles are not 'natural', but are assigned because of underpinning beliefs and practices.

On our wander through the centuries, we shall look at where ideas and beliefs about male superiority come from, and how they are linked to 'tradition'. Tradition is about ideas, beliefs and practices handed down from generation to generation. The ways by which these ideas are created, sustained and continued are as a consequence of a three-part process beginning with ideas, then discourse, which defines and explains the ideas, and ultimately practice, which becomes the 'norm' and, ultimately, tradition. So, where did ideas about woman and man come from? What has been said about women and about men? How have certain ideas about women and men become so pervasive? Is there any truth in them? How are they linked to patriarchy?

As we consider the ways in which woman and man have been explained, described and constructed in the social world, we discover that what has been said about woman – the discourse – has led to a social construction of woman as everything a man is not. Since ancient times, man has been defined and explained using positive words to describe his characteristics – and temperament (such as 'strong', 'intelligent', 'independent', 'leader', 'warrior' and 'provider'); whilst woman has been assigned the opposite, negative, characteristics (for example, 'weak', 'simple', 'in need of guidance and protection' and 'dependent'). Men assigned to themselves every positive human characteristic and assigned to women the polar opposites. These characteristics underpin stereotypical images of women and of men. We shall see that these stereotypes have a long history and continue to exist in the modern world.

Historically, patriarchal societies and organisation have perpetuated these stereotypes. In patriarchal societies, the overriding aim is for some men to regulate and control other men and all women and children. Women and men are expected to conform to fixed gender identities, based on stereotypical images of 'masculinity' and 'femininity'. The socialisation into particular beliefs and 'truths', roles and responsibilities is a form of 'interior colonisation' (a belief in the 'natural order' of sexual differences), which is more effective than any form of segregation or stratification and is more uniform and enduring. It is also the least expensive form of control. The traditional patriarchal discourse on sexual differences underpins both historical and current relationships of dominance and subordination. It is a relationship of power.

> Sexual domination obtains nevertheless as perhaps the most pervasive ideology of our culture and provides its most fundamental concept of power.[2]

Historically, the world religions have played a major part in perpetuating these stereotypes. Prior to the Enlightenment and the Scientific Revolution, humans attempted to explain the world through myths and magic. Religious 'truths' played a major role in this; from the ancient world with its myriad of gods to later a belief in the 'one God' of the three main world religions, Judaism, Christianity and Islam. Similar discourses about men and women, temperament, roles and status exist in each of these Abrahamic religions, not least through association with the story of Genesis. Each of these religions is organised around patriarchy; men play the key roles, while women are mere observers. Our focus here is on Christianity, which influenced European thought.

Stereotypical images of men and women have encompassed the globe through secular and religious 'truths' about woman and about man. Religions, together with patriarchal states, have ensured the perpetuation of traditional ideas, discourse and practice. Christianity offers a clear continuity of ideas from the ancient world to the present; and has been instrumental in the ideas, beliefs, traditions, law and organisation of the Western secular world. At the outset, we shall examine whether the characteristics assigned to women and to men are valid. Is it possible that women and men are so different? Are women and men confined by their biology? Are the roles assigned to men and women 'natural'? Do *all* men exhibit all of the positive characteristics assigned to them as a group? Do *all* women exhibit all of the negative characteristics assigned to them as a group?

Over the twentieth century, research has shown that the possibilities of innate temperamental differences (characteristics) are remote, and no definite equation between nature and temperament has emerged. The character of gender – that is, personality structure in terms of sexual category (male or female) – appears to be cultural rather than biological in character. 'Core gender identity' is established in infancy, and appears strongly influenced by socialisation. As early as the 1960s, research with intersex patients showed that gender is determined by postnatal forces, regardless of the anatomy or physiology of the external genitalia. It is more likely that 'masculinity' and 'femininity' are socially constructed within the individual, rather than absolute biological givens.[3] That this socialisation continues as a universal condition through acquired value systems indicates the strength of patriarchy and its resistance to biological and psychological evidence which undermines its ideology.

Feminist scholarship has pointed out that patriarchy, as a governing ideology, prevents men as well as women from developing and experiencing their full humanity; and both sexes are prevented from developing their full potential. The success of patriarchal ideology, with its mutually exclusive, contradictory and polar qualities of categories of 'masculinity' and 'femininity', limits male and female personalities to only half of their human potential and allows for a limited range of activities. Patriarchy represents a power division between men and women, and between some men and less powerful men, based on sex and sexual stereotypes. The aim is conformity to traditional patriarchal ideas. Control of some men, all women and children operates at two levels; it occurs in the public world and in private, in the home. These sites are mutually supportive. Public patriarchy is based principally in public sites, such as commercial and state institutions. The principal strategy is that of segregation and subordination. Men and women are segregated into separate groups by men in power. Some groups have more power than others; some men control and subordinate other groups of men and most women; and some groups never meet, due to economic, social or political reasons.

At the private level, patriarchal society, organisation and religions provide justification for the operation of private patriarchy by individual patriarchs. In the family, some men use the same strategies used at the public level to control and subordinate the younger men, women and children in the household. Individual patriarchs demand that women fulfil their 'natural' roles of material and sexual services to men. At the public level, patriarchal society, organisation and religions affirm the private patriarch, segregate, exclude and subordinate women.[4]

Strategies of exclusion have been, and continue to be, employed in the public and private spheres in order to further control women. However, while some men have been damaged by patriarchy, they do at least have the possibility to reach a position of power themselves; women, on the other hand, are denied such a possibility simply because they are women. Women have been hedged in with taboos and rituals, which have served to exclude them from full participation in society.

As we shall see later, these taboos are often associated with women's natural functions, especially blood and childbirth and the denigration of women's sexual organs. Central to both public and private patriarchy is the control of women's sexuality, most especially the control of reproduction. Marie Louise Janssen-Jurriet (1982) considers that

> The quintessence of patriarchy is the male control of reproduction which is orientated to maximise the security of the individual paterfamilias, the oldest member of the clan, the chieftain or the men of the ruling social classes.[5]

The control of reproduction has been and continues to be of concern to societies, religious leaders and patriarchs. Central to this concern is the felt need to control sexual activity, which is associated with passion, lust and sin. The human sex drive, considered as 'an unruly passion' in need of control, has been hedged in with prohibitions, which have attempted to control sexual activity and women's generative capacity. We shall return later to this issue. Traditional ideas about reproduction and morality provide security for the economic foundations and organisation of patriarchy. Patriarchs have strong motives to want to control women and reproduction. If men are to retain their power, they have an interest in the production of the next generation, which maximises the security of the nation, the clan, the family and the patriarch. If men are to maintain patriarchal institutions, they must develop sex-specific solidarity structures. In order to win allies in the next generation, male children must be convinced of the insignificance of women and of motherhood. This is achieved through processes of socialisation, especially through initiation rites, which exclude women and alienate boys from their mothers. The older men shape the identity of the boys in a system of communication and meaning from which they exclude women. Membership of men's organisations is dependent on these systems. Through these systems and consequent male-dominated structures a male, hierarchical elite re-enforces its position of power over subordinates – that is, over other men, all women and children.

Apart from biological and religious justifications for patriarchy, one of the most effective weapons in maintaining male superiority has been that of exclusion. In the state, women have been excluded from public life, from education and from employment. In the religious setting women have been excluded from full participation in worship and doctrine. In patriarchal religions the public segregation and control of women is evident in the refusal to allow women access to sacred spaces; worship alongside men; to preach or teach; or to hold any position of power. Some men are subject to the power of religious patriarchs, not through exclusion, but through control of their sexuality – for example, the Catholic priesthood. The role of the celibate male will be considered in a later chapter, where it will become evident that the institution of celibacy in the Catholic Christian Church is an apparatus of power, the backbone of a patriarchal Church.

The weapon of exclusion also removed women from history. Apart from a few notable exceptions, history has focused on the deeds of men; and in so doing has eliminated the social and political history of half of humanity. A male history, together with its associated myths, is the basis of 'traditions' and culture in society, as they attempt to deal with the meanings of events and of existence. History and myths have supported and sustained beliefs in male supremacy;[6] together with tradition and religion, they continue to corroborate and justify existing roles, responsibilities and traditions in the present and establish rights and duties of the sexes.

Religious myths, especially those associated with the original creation of the human race – in Judaism, Christianity and Islam – have played a significant part in explaining and justifying male superiority. The myth of Adam and Eve established the rights and duties of the sexes in all three Abrahamic religions. Women have been excluded from religious systems of communication, meaning and spiritual property, which have been controlled and handed down by men. Women's spirituality has been denied or ignored. Viewed through a prism of sexuality, women have

21

been confirmed as sexual and domestic servants to men. An examination of the male history of the early Christian Church shows that women's social and political contributions to early Christianity have been either downplayed or eliminated.[7] The women who have been mentioned in history tend to be virgins or women who 'chose' death instead of being raped.

Philosophical, medical and religious beliefs about procreation place men in the primary role, even as co-creator with God, while women appear only as the vessel for man's 'seed'. Later we shall examine how the story of Adam and Eve led to the association of woman with sex and sin in the doctrine of 'original sin'; and to the myth of a prelapsarian purity, which could be accessed only by the continent male.

In patriarchal, monotheistic religions, legitimacy for male claims to superiority was established through the primacy of the male God. Male religious leaders continue to hold the exclusive right to explain the meaning of human existence; the interpretation of religious meaning; and the recording of religious beliefs and practices for entire communities. This presumed right continues to depend on the 'truth' of religious myths and 'tradition'. While women may not accept all male judgements, the male interpretation of religious meaning affects their lives through purity rules, taboos and rituals of conduct towards men, which express women's subordination in religion and in patriarchal societies. The continued use of exclusive language, especially in reference to the male God, and the association of women with sex and sin, reinforces the idea of the biological and spiritual inferiority of women. A woman is merely the vessel for nurturing a man's child.

Patriarchal religions do not exist in a vacuum. Patriarchal religion and the patriarchal state are mutually supportive and sustaining. It is unsurprising that with the rise of political authorities, and the rise of the nation state, the state became the guarantor of patriarchal power. As in patriarchal religions, there are command posts of power in the state which are usually held by men – in economics, the armed forces, the political system, the judiciary, structures and organisation. The patriarchal state controls the public sphere. In private, the family becomes the microcosm, a mirror image of the patriarchal state; it is the building block of society. The private patriarch controls the sexual impulses of the individual, and the father's total control over sons, daughters and wives serves to internally maintain the order of the state; the stability of which is dependent on a rigorous hierarchy, and the strict compliance to command and obedience.

Historically, the patriarchal state and religions have been concerned with the control of women's bodies and reproduction. Women have had few rights to divorce, to extramarital relations, to the legitimisation of out-of-wedlock children, to marriages based on love or choice, to contraception or to abortion. Women who did not conform were (and in some cases continue to be) punished severely. This control of women and their bodies has a long history. Long before the Christian era, Sumerian, Assyrian and Babylonian codices made abortion a criminal offence.[8] In Hindu law, abortion made a woman an outcast.[9] In Western liberal democracies, while the ideology of patriarchy remains, it is to some extent muted and women have become accustomed to making decisions about their sexual relations and fertility for themselves. Nevertheless, some women have to deal with the inherent contradictions between what is acceptable in the society in which they live and what is acceptable in terms of a patriarchal religion or a private patriarch. Much male control of women's bodies centres on the issue of contraception and abortion. In the twenty-first century some states, religions and private patriarchs continue to support each other in preventing women from accessing family-planning and abortion services.

Historically, one of the main justifications for the control of reproduction was concerning who was responsible for new life – man or woman? Prior to the age of the male God there is evidence that women were revered, and their fertility respected. Feminist and biblical scholarship has outlined the gradual move from the notion of a 'Great Mother' God to that of a male God and the consequential downgrading of women.[10] There would have come a time when it dawned on men that there was a

23

link between copulation and birth. It was this awareness that began the process of the male appropriation of reproduction. Woman was gradually removed from the position of primary initiator of new life; man became the primary source of new life; woman was merely a 'flowerpot 'or 'propagator' for the man's 'seed'.[11] The decline of the age of the Great Mother and the rise of the phallus will be considered in more detail in later chapters. The belief that man held the primary role in procreation has been a major underpinning in the justification for male superiority; and has been significant in supporting and sustaining patriarchy. Much attention has been given to the rise of the phallus and phallic symbols, but the phallus is merely a dispenser for semen, *our* attention focuses on the ejaculate – semen.

In summary, this chapter has defined and briefly outlined what is meant by patriarchy – that is, a universal scheme of domination by birthright. Links have been made between patriarchal ideas about women and men that have led to discursive practice. Traditional stereotypes of what it is to be 'woman' and 'man' are fundamental to the roles and responsibilities assigned to each sex and are at the foundation of patriarchal beliefs and organisation. Patriarchal societies and religions are mutually supportive and sustaining. Both justify the subordination and exclusion of women, which in turn justifies the private patriarch who acts in the interest of religion and the state.

The quintessence of patriarchy is male control of women, their bodies and reproduction. Women are confined to specific roles and responsibilities, which focus on service to men, arising from the stereotypical characteristics assigned to women. Patriarchy has been perpetuated through male history, secular and religious myths, and the exclusion of women from history. The decline of the age of the Great Mother and the rise of the phallus are subjects of recent historical scholarship. The rise of the male God and the phallus is linked to the fantasies surrounding semen. These fantasies go some way to understanding why man believed (and some continue to believe) he was a superior form of humanity. A paradigm shift occurred as man appropriated the primary role in the creation of new life.

The myths and beliefs of Ancient Greece and Imperial Rome, together with the Hebrew Bible, formed the matrix of European thought. It has been through these myths that patriarchal ideas have been perpetuated in the Western world. We are looking for the continuity of these ideas and practices over the past 2,000 years. We shall examine the impact of Greek thought, the organisation of Imperial Rome and the ideas, discourse and practices of the Christian Church. Together, these have supported and sustained both public and private patriarchy in the Western world. We shall then move on to consider the decline of the age of the Great Mother and the rise of the phallus.

The trail of semen wends its way through the early Christian Church as a patriarchal organisation emerges. Sexual theology supports 'common sense' ideas about woman and man and provide legitimacy for religious and social arrangements that have controlled women over 2,000 years. Finally, we ask if patriarchy continues to exist in the twenty-first century. Do patriarchal ideas about women continue to exist and have meaning? Do traditional ideas continue to define women and their role? Some women have experienced the mitigation of the worst effects of patriarchy, particularly in the Western world; however, the belief that women and men are on an evolving cultural journey towards equality is misguided (Campbell, 2013). The evidence is that progress towards equality in many parts of the world has stopped, even if it had ever begun. A new era of patriarchy has emerged in which violence has proliferated; self-hatred has flourished, violence against women, sexual abuse, especially rape, is committed daily with impunity and sex trafficking thrives.

CHAPTER TWO:

SEMEN: THE MISSING LINK

An examination of ancient texts reveals that biological explanations about semen underpin notions of male superiority. These biological explanations provide justification for notions of man's superiority, and man's appropriation of the primary role in procreation. Arguments for male superiority rest in the fantasies surrounding semen. These fantasies articulated by the Greeks (in particular Galen the physician and Aristotle, the supposed first 'scientific' observer) provided an explanation for man's superior nature. They supported and sustained the social, political and cultural arrangements of public and private patriarchy, later advanced in the European world. In these ancient discourses, the male ejaculate – semen – became elevated to a liquid that contained within it all that was required for new life. Semen contained the whole foetus in embryo and woman was merely the receptacle for man's 'seed'.

The belief in the primary role of semen in procreation has been shared, supported and sustained by patriarchal religions. Judaism, as the original Abrahamic religion, played an important role in the perceptions of woman and man – perceptions later adopted by Christianity. The third Abrahamic religion influenced by Judaism was Islam.

A reverence for semen was evident in Judaism. The sin of Onan involved masturbation 'spilling the seed onto the ground'. The most authoritative work of Jewish law states categorically that

> It is forbidden to release semen for no purpose and this is as serious a sin as any in the Torah . . . those who masturbate . . . and release semen, not only is it a serious sin . . . but it is as though they've killed a human being.[1]

In the Hindu religion, a devout Hindu who did not have intercourse with his wife during her fertile period was described as an embryo killer. In Christianity, ejaculation of semen into any other vessel other than the womb was considered seriously sinful. In later Christian sexual theology, masturbation was conflated to a sin worse than murder, rape and sexual assault.

Over time, many cultures had fantasies associated with semen. In Qigong and Chinese medicine, semen was an 'essence', a sexual energy in a man that reduces each time it is ejaculated. In Papua New Guinea, some communities believed that semen of older men could bestow manliness and wisdom to the younger men; and for this, the men needed to fellate their elders to receive their authority and powers. One wonders how that idea took root. No ancient society seemed clear about what semen was, where it came from or what it consisted of, but this did not stop the fantastic stories surrounding semen from becoming the accepted 'truth' in particular societies. In ancient Eastern cultures, gemstones were believed to be drops of divine semen. Jade was the dried semen of the celestial dragon. In Greece, Pythagoreans believed that semen came from the brain. Aristotle said that the area around the eyes carried the best seeds or *sperm* and semen should not be wasted.[2]

These 'truths' are easily challenged, but the belief that semen contained the whole foetus in embryo, which justified man's primary position in procreation, also led to social traditions and cultural arrangements that continue to use and abuse women. In this, the Western world is also culpable, for the beliefs of the ancient world formed the foundations of European, and later Western civilisation. The ancient world – that is, the area around the Mediterranean basin, in particular Greece – is widely accepted as the cradle of Western civilisation. The beliefs about the creation of man and woman recorded in the

Hebrew Bible were also a major influence in the presumptions of male superiority. This cultural milieu provides us with our first staging post, because 'common sense' notions of the day reveal that the discourse about semen led to the presumed superiority of the male and provided the rationale and legitimacy for patriarchy, which affected the development of cultural norms, values and religious doctrines. The ways in which woman and man were defined and explained are significant because ideas lead to action and action to tradition. Woman as man's 'inferior other' became the 'truth', the 'norm', and social, political and religious organisation underpinned this patriarchal construction of woman and man.

The discourse on semen supports the practice of patriarchy, and beliefs about semen and male power are inextricably linked to the philosophical and cultural discussion of Ancient Greece. An examination of the writings of Aristotle, Plato, Galen the physician and Homer (the cultural and philosophical discourses of the Greek, and, later, Roman world) provides us with a clear picture of 'woman' and 'man'. The centrality of semen in the discourse cannot be denied. These ancient beliefs about semen provide the *missing link* in theories about male superiority and patriarchal organisation. This is not a just another *theory* in line with easily disprovable theories about man's superiority (all men are stronger than all women, only men are the warriors, the hunters and so on); it is an indisputable, now proven *fact*.

Significant secular and religious discourses from the ancient world provide the cultural and philosophical context of the countries around the Mediterranean; we can trace these ideas in an unbroken line from the ancient world to the twenty-first century. Our main focus is on Europe and the impact of Greek, Roman and Christian thought on Western civilisation. There are some similarities with other parts of the world, particularly those countries that adopted European thought and values. There are also some similarities between Christianity, Judaism and Islam, but these similarities are not examined here.

This is a seminal moment – no pun intended – as beliefs about semen are exposed as the biological justification for beliefs about male superiority. Greek philosophical, biological and medical discourse provides a fascinating insight to the contemporary beliefs about male superiority which contributed to later European thought. In these discourses, the Greek discourse about semen is central; it provides 'biological evidence' for man's superiority. The mere ownership of a phallus was insufficient to make a man a man; a man must have a sufficient supply of semen. According to Galen[3], the Greek physician, the possession of semen made men 'virile, hot, well-built, deep-voiced, strong in thought and deed'. It was through the possession of semen that men were able to think, reason, define and explain truth; it was semen that gave men the ability to act, to organise, to fight. Man, described later by Michel Foucault[4] as the 'spermatic animal par excellence', was not merely superior to women, but was superior to all other forms of life. The possession of semen and resulting fantasies surrounding semen provided a 'biological basis' for all the positive characteristics assigned to men and led to the legitimisation of man's domination of women, children and the natural world.

The negative characteristics assigned to women derived from their lack of semen. According to Galen, the lack of 'vital spirit' (semen) in women 'made them [women] more soft, more liquid, more clammy-cold, altogether more formless than men'. Lacking semen, woman was mentally and physically weak. Woman's physical weakness meant that man was needed to protect her; unable to act alone, she must have a man as her guide. Unable to think clearly or logically, woman had to depend on man to define and explain philosophical, social and religious 'truths'. Aristotle, lauded for centuries as the first 'scientific' observer, said that the male was 'naturally' superior to the female; the inequality was a permanent factor due to her 'deliberative faculty', being 'without authority much like a child's'[5]. Although Aristotle's work has been praised as an early example of scientific observation, when it came to observing women, Aristotle's 'scientific observation' unfortunately gave way to prejudice. In his *History of Animals*, he recorded that

29

a menstruating woman could make a mirror turn 'bloody dark like a cloud', because the menstrual blood passed through her eyes to the surface of the mirror. Aristotle also observed that women had fewer teeth than men.

The Greek philosophical, biological and medical discourses were mutually supportive. The possession of semen not only gave men positive physical, psychological and mental characteristics, but also gave men the primary role in procreation. Aristotle asserted that the male semen was the major factor in the conception of a child. It was assumed that the male 'seed' contained the entire foetus in embryo; a woman's function was simply to act as an incubator for the man's child. According to Aretaeus, nature intended all foetuses to be male. Males were those foetuses that had realised their full potential – to become male. He used the possession of semen as his evidence. For the foetus to be successful, it had to amass a surplus of 'heat' or 'vital spirit' in the womb. Aretaeus gave the ejaculation of male seed as the proof for this.

> For it is the semen, when possessed of vitality, which makes us men, hot, well-braced in limbs, heavy, well-voiced, spirited, strong to think and act.[6]

If enough 'vital spirit' did not come to the foetus in the womb, a female child – i.e. a 'failed male' – would result. I did not find any discussion on how the human race would continue if all foetuses fulfilled their potential. It would appear that the idea was not followed through to its logical conclusion. However, this notion of woman as a 'failed male' had a long shelf life in European thought. Woman was considered not fully human. In some parts of the world, this idea persists in the twenty-first century.

The physician Galen[7] also considered 'vital heat' necessary in the development of the foetus. Those foetuses which had not received enough 'vital heat' in the womb resulted in female children. He concluded that women could not retain 'vital heat' due to the periodic loss of surplus heat through menstruation.

Periodic menstruation demonstrated that women could not burn up surplus heat, which then coagulated within them. There was, however, a dilemma; this surplus heat was needed for the development of the foetus. Presumably, during pregnancy women retained enough 'vital heat' to nurture the foetus. Galen does not go on to consider the possibility that woman might have purposely been designed by nature to play an equal part in procreation, even though he warned that if these surpluses were not for the nurture of the foetus, men might think that a creator would not purposely make half the whole race imperfect and, as it were, mutilated unless there was to be some great advantage in such a mutilation.

What is clear in the philosophical and medical discourses of the time is that evidence was not a requirement to define and explain 'truth'. The ways that women were discussed were subjective and prejudicial, and suggested a hatred and fear of women, their sexuality and their bodies. Galen, taking the male as the 'norm' (naturally), decided that women were men turned inside out; the ovaries were 'smaller, less perfect testes'[8]. Plato's comments on the male and female sexual organs reveal evidence of misogyny as a factor in biological explanations about man, woman and reproduction.[9] The penis is described in positive terms – 'masterful' – whilst the uterus is described in negative terms as a 'revolting animal within an animal'. Plato also explained that the womb was like the penis, which 'becomes rebellious and masterful, like an animal, disobedient to reason and maddened with the sting of lust'.

Within these discourses, the centrality of semen cannot be denied. These discourses provided 'evidence' for biological differences between men and women. The fantasies surrounding semen were instrumental in the patriarchal construction of woman and of man, and consequently, the construction of masculinity and femininity, the presumption of male superiority, the justification for patriarchy, the control of women and children, and the use and abuse of women as servants and sexual objects. Many of these ideas persist in the modern world.

CHAPTER THREE:

EVE THE TEMPTRESS, ADAM THE WIMP

One of the earliest religious justifications for the subordination of women was provided by the Hebrew Bible and the Creation stories, in which woman was clearly identified as man's helpmate and subordinate to him. As Christianity developed out of Judaism it took with it traditional ideas about women and about men. Around 500 years later, the new religion of Islam also accepted many of these traditional ideas. These three Abrahamic religions carried forward many ideas from the Hebrew Bible, which provided 'divine' justification for ideas about women and about men. Genesis 2 and 3 have been used as 'proof' that woman should be subordinate to man.

Some feminists reject the Bible because it is anti-women. Feminist biblical scholarship has suggested that traditional explanations for Genesis were speculative and strongly influenced by patriarchal Hebrew society. The goal of feminist theology has been to illustrate alternative readings of Genesis in which there is equality among men and women, not superiority of either sex over the other.[1] Feminist critics have challenged Christian interpretations of the Creation stories. For example, Carol Meyers considers that Genesis 2–3 is a 'wisdom tale' that attempts to address the complexities of human life.[2] Recent scholarship continues its uphill battle to offer alternative readings of Genesis 2–3, not least because the story of the serpent and Eve, the eating of the forbidden fruit, has long been used to justify the naivety, wickedness and seductiveness of women.[3, 4] The Hebrew Creation story is a significant staging post worthy of examination, because Augustine later linked Adam and Eve's downfall to the sexual act and subsequently to original sin; and Aquinas elevated semen to the 'divine'.

The Creation story in the Hebrew Bible was an attempt to explain how the world was created. It was rightly assumed that the world had developed over time, and humans had been one of the last to develop. In the absence of the later understanding of evolution, the Hebrews constructed an explanation that involved their notion of a monotheistic God. They believed in a former 'perfect world' which had somehow been contaminated and despoiled. In simple terms, the Hebrew explanation for Creation is that God took six days to create the world; then he completed his task by creating man. God took the seventh day off. Surprisingly, the God who had managed to create the universe realised that he had not thought this last bit through. He noticed that man was lonely, so he decided to create woman, not as man had been created but from a part of man's body – his rib. Man and woman lived in the most beautiful and wonderful place, called Paradise. The man and woman, later named Adam and Eve, enjoyed life and 'Everything in the garden was perfect.' Then everything changed. Why? What happened? The story explains: there was a serpent (who was really the Devil), which snaked its way around the garden looking for an opening to get back at God for throwing him out of heaven. He found it! There was one fruit tree in the garden, the fruit of which the man and woman must not eat. The serpent persuaded Eve to eat from the tree. Eve then persuaded Adam to eat from the tree. God was not pleased and punished them by throwing them out of the garden.

The context of this tale is significant, because, according to the story, if it had not been for a woman we would all still be enjoying life in Paradise. A perfect Creation had been spoiled. This spoliation and exodus from Paradise was entirely the woman's fault. The inference is that Adam was minding his own business when Eve sidled up to him and put the idea of eating the forbidden fruit into his head. He clearly needed little persuasion. Nevertheless, it was Eve's fault. Eve had tempted Adam into disobeying God. When God challenged Adam and Eve about what they had done, Adam said in effect that it was Eve's fault as 'She gave me of the tree, and I did eat.' Nothing was said in the story about joint responsibility or that Adam should have dissuaded Eve. It was a story biased in favour of Adam. Eve got the blame. Barrister Helena Kennedy's book *Eve was Framed* (1994) says it all in its title; shame she was not there to defend Eve at the time.

God made it clear that Adam and Eve were cast out of Paradise. They would now have to work for their living. The woman had spoiled it for the whole human race. Eve was picked out for special attention. She and all her descendants would bring forth children in pain as an extra punishment. Adam had been dragged down with her; if she had not persuaded him to eat the fruit, everything would have remained perfect. In summary, God created the world and in this world was a place called Paradise. Man was created in order to enjoy Paradise. Woman was a mere afterthought created for man's benefit. Eve was tempted by the Devil; she then tempted Adam, who could not resist her pleas. They were expelled from Paradise. Adam, Eve and their descendants would have to work for a living, but Eve would have the extra burden of pain in childbearing, because the loss of Paradise had been her fault. Adam, not man enough to accept his share of the blame, is revealed as a wimp. The story did not help the image of the serpent either.

In the early Christian Church the patriarchal interpretation of Genesis 2–3 was evident in Corinthians[5] when Paul points out that 'Neither was man created for woman, but woman was created for man.' Tertullian, one of the earliest Christian theologians and a polemicist against *heresy*, especially Christian Gnosticism, spoke to women saying:

> And do you not know that you are each an Eve? . . . you are the devil's gateway: you are the unsealer of that tree: you are the first deserter of the divine law: you are she who persuaded him whom the devil was not valiant enough to attack. You destroyed so easily, God's image man.[6]

We shall see in a later chapter that this negative view of women was re-enforced by the three 'Fathers of the Church' Augustine, Albert and Aquinas. By the time of the Reformation (early sixteenth to the mid-seventeenth centuries), the patriarchal view of women is firmly entrenched in Christian theology. Martin Luther, a German theologian whose challenges to practices in the Christian Church contributed to the Protestant Reformation, did not challenge the literal 'truth' of the Creation myth. There was no Reformation for women. Luther preached that 'Satan's cleverness is perceived also in this, that he attacks the weak part of the human nature, Eve the woman, not Adam the man.'[7]

Following the Reformation, the hegemony of Christendom was destroyed. The Catholic Christian Church claimed absolute legitimacy; it was able to trace its mandate from Christ himself through papal succession. The various Protestant Churches that emerged from the Reformation felt that their mandate was as legitimate as that of the orthodox Catholic Church. What did not change on either side of the schism was the patriarchal interpretation of Genesis with regard to women.

The reality is that over time Eve has been the villain of the piece purely through speculation and by an interpretation influenced by patriarchal beliefs. Man left alone would be perfect. It was a woman who tempted man to evil; therefore man must be wary of woman for she is a temptress and will lead him astray. Men must control women, otherwise women will be their downfall. Cultural and social life is full of contradictions and this attitude towards women is difficult to reconcile with expectations laid on women to take responsibility for controlling male desire. We shall return to this story later when we discuss how Christian theologians made some interesting additions.

CHAPTER FOUR:

STEREOTYPES AS A WEAPON

At this point it is useful to pause and consider the traditional, patriarchal, stereotypical images of man and of woman, because one of the most effective weapons in the arsenal of socialisation into particular male or female characteristics, roles and responsibilities is that of gender stereotypes. Currently, in the wake of a confused attempt at political correctness, the term 'gender' has become synonymous with man and woman; it has replaced the word 'sex'. Sex means male or female. Gender relates to the biological, mental and social characteristics assigned to women and men.

The formation of stereotypical images of any kind is based on the beliefs and needs of the dominant group. Stereotypical gender images of 'masculinity' and 'femininity' are based firstly on what men admire most in themselves: aggression, intelligence and efficiency. Femininity is based on the opposite characteristics to masculinity – that is, passivity, ignorance and ineffectiveness. In traditional patriarchal societies, man has been socially constructed as strong, intelligent, trustworthy, reliable, logical and able to take decisions, together with a plethora of other positive characteristics. Woman on the other hand has been socially constructed with opposite and negative characteristics: weak, simple, untrustworthy, illogical, a ditherer, plus a wide range of other negative characteristics. However, if these characteristics are to be accepted as 'natural', 'normal' and 'true' in a modern scientific world they require legitimation. Proof is required. Religious justification is insufficient and requires examination.

It is important to understand why men assume all positions of importance worldwide. It is because gender characteristics are believed to be 'natural' and 'normal'. Men, by virtue of their reputed greater intelligence, aggression and efficacy, assign to themselves all positions of power. Women, by virtue of their supposed ignorance, passivity, ineffectiveness and biology, are assigned roles designed to service men both materially and sexually. It is assumed that men are more suited to power due to their 'natural' abilities. Women are expected to do the caring for children and vulnerable adults, service men's sexual needs and accept men as their 'natural' masters. Patriarchal societies and popular attitudes presume that these psychosocial gender distinctions are based on biological differences between the sexes. Cultural arrangements and roles are assumed merely cooperating with nature, and to attempt to alter sex-role assignments is seen as contrary to the natural and divine order.[1] Legitimacy for these 'natural' characteristics is rooted in the fantasies surrounding semen. The male discourse on semen is a key factor in stereotypical images of masculinity and femininity. Man, socially constructed with positive characteristics, is the sexual animal par excellence.[2] Woman, socially constructed as man's inferior 'other', has only one useful role – that is, to service man's physical and sexual needs while man is busy ruling the universe.[3]

Culture and religion have emphasised that a woman's primary role is to service men and to bear children. Traditionally, women have been expected to have one sexual partner, a husband. She should provide him with a constant outlet for his (presumed) uncontrollable sexual urges. Accepted 'common sense' is that a man 'will look elsewhere' if he is not satisfied at home. Consequently, if a man does look elsewhere for sex he cannot be blamed as an unaccommodating wife drove him to it. Women are not expected to have the same sexual urges as men. Those women who have more than one sexual partner are not offered the same excuse and are described in negative terms.

In the discourse on semen, it is evident that it is not enough for a man to be male; a man has to look and act male. A man must not merely possess all positive characteristics to be a 'man', but he must demonstrate them. The medical discourses reveal that one of the things men feared most was that of becoming 'womanish'. A man's 'heat' and 'vital spirit' might cool, leading a man to approach the state of a woman. The physician Galen suggested that lack of heat from childhood could cause the male body to collapse back into a state of un-differentiation.[4] If the vital heat was to maintain its effectiveness it was never enough to be male – a man had to strive to remain 'virile', he had to exclude all signs of 'softness' which might suggest his loss of manhood. Consequently, effeminate characteristics were to be feared. Peter Brown illustrates this concern.

> The small-town notables . . . noted a man's walk . . . reacted to the rhythms of his speech . . . listened attentively to the tell-tale resonance of his voice. Any of these might betray the ominous loss of a hot, high-spirited momentum, a flagging of the clear-cut self-restraint, and a relaxing of the taut elegance of voice and gesture that made a man a man, the unruffled master of the subject world.[5]

Man had to be seen to be a man, master of the universe. Macho man was born.

Images of masculinity are more to do with supporting male power than they are to do with what it means to be a 'man'. The concern for male power is thrown into relief with the question of homosexual activity. The underlying concern in male same-sex activity was loss of male power through becoming identified with women. In Greece, a marked degree of tolerance was accorded to men on the matter of homosexuality. That men might wish to caress or penetrate other beautiful men was of little surprise. What the doctors and townsfolk could not understand or accept was that the pursuit of pleasure might lead some men to demean themselves by playing the female role. Concern about homosexual relations centred on the breakdown of the strict hierarchical structure between the sexes rather than on the sexual act itself. Thus, the fantasies surrounding semen contributed to the fear of 'loss of manhood'. The loss of 'heat' and 'vital spirit' would lead to 'womanishness' and, with this, the 'natural' power of man by virtue of his possession of semen would be lost. The protection of 'vital heat' – that is, semen – became a major preoccupation.[6]

Socially constructed as man's 'inferior other', woman was described as a mistake of nature, biologically and intellectually inferior, a 'misbegotten man'. These notions of women's mental incapacity have existed for at least several thousand years. In classical Greek culture, the male was active, identified with civilisation, reason and order; woman was passive, identified with nature, emotion and chaos. Only men could apply reason and logic to life, to control emotion and instinct; women were subject to impulse and selfishness. In Hebrew law, women, children and slaves were classified together, because they had 'light flighty minds'. The 'natural' incapacity of women justified male domination.[7]

In the Roman world in the first century BC, the Roman jurist Cicero argued that 'Because of their weakness of intellect, all women should be under the power of a male.' In the third century AD, Ulpian asserted that guardians were necessary for women 'on account of the weakness of their sex and of their ignorance in business matters'. The 'levity of mind' of all women (except the six Vestal Virgins) meant that women and their children must be under a man's guardianship.[8] Male control of women was gradually legitimised by the law. In Roman law 'paternal power' gave the father sole and absolute authority over his wife and children. The paterfamilias had the power of life and death over all members of his family. In constructing women as biologically and intellectually inferior, men provided themselves with legitimate reasons to control women and their bodies.[9]

A further factor in men's felt need to control women was their fear of women and the power of sexuality – a fear which was well established in the world from which Christianity was to spring. Hatred and fear of women and their natural processes can be found in Greek literature, Christian theology and Roman ideas and organisation,[10] which together were the foundations of European thought and laws. It is necessary therefore to consider what was contained within these discourses. In Homer's writings (fifth century BC), the image of the Goddess embodies men's fears that unless female power is controlled by male principle women will be dangerous to men. The desirability of their ultimate subordination can be seen in the figure of Hera in the *Iliad*. She embodies female beauty and sexual power. The male god Zeus, fearful for his power, struggles and ultimately wins out over her.[11] Fear of women and of sexuality is later echoed in early Christian sources and is clear to see in several of the Gnostic gospels[12], which were circulating up until the Council of Nicaea, after which the Gospels of Matthew, Mark, Luke and John became the foundational books of the New Testament. In the 'Dialogue of the Saviour', Jesus warns his disciples to 'Pray where there is no woman . . . [and to] destroy the works of femaleness'. The 'works of femaleness' are apparently the activities of intercourse and procreation. Elaine Pagels (1990) argues that in each of these cases the target is not women but the power of sexuality.[12]

Whereas the male ejaculate was described positively as the 'vital spirit' that made a man a man, women's natural functions were denigrated and led to the stigmatisation of menstruating women and girls. Menstrual taboos set women apart and disbarred them from full participation in society. These taboos continue in some societies in the twenty-first century. The strength and persistence of the taboos demonstrates not only ignorance, but also the high level of fear and danger associated with menstrual blood and its uncontrollable nature. Some Eastern cultures have long held that

> A woman in her courses is not to gaze upon the sacred fire, sit in water, behold the sun, or hold conversation with a man.[13]

In some societies a woman continues to be excluded from normal social life when menstruating. Ideas about pollution and blood contributed to the denigration of a woman's role in intercourse and conception and to notions of uncleanness associated with childbirth. *The Book of Thomas the Contender* in the Nag Hammadi Library[14] warns, 'Woe to you who love intimacy with womankind, and polluted intercourse with it.' Nature is described in *The Paraphrase of Shem* as a horror who

> turned her dark vagina and cast from her the power of fire, which was in her from the beginning, through the practice of darkness.[15]

A fear of women and of the power of sexuality, prejudice against women and notions of uncleanness associated with menstrual blood and childbirth all contributed to beliefs about women in the world from which Christianity sprang. The prejudicial descriptions of women had overwhelmed any positive descriptions of the female gods venerated for their fecundity.

Images of masculinity and femininity, role and status do not appear to be a constant in human nature. Physical or intellectual strength, for example, does not constitute a sufficient explanation for male supremacy, for all men are neither physically nor intellectually stronger than all women. Therefore male superiority cannot be assumed inevitable on physiological grounds; it is more likely to be the result of the acceptance by society of stereotypical gender characteristics. Here is something that you can try, which I have done over many years of teaching with almost every cohort of students. First, make a list of stereotypical male characteristics – strong, intelligent, decisive, brave, dependable and so on. Then make a list of the opposite characteristics to these positive characteristics. It becomes clear that woman has been given the opposite, negative, characteristics to the positive characteristics that men assigned to themselves. Woman is weak, dim, dependent, in need of protection, unreliable and so on. Then ask yourself if you 'fit' the stereotype. I have yet to meet a student who has not assigned to themselves some characteristics of each stereotype at some times during their lives. The reality – the 'truth' – is that as human beings we can demonstrate all of these characteristics at certain times because of life experiences. As man or woman, we are more alike than we are different.

Second, make another list that illustrates different attitudes towards male and female sexual behaviour. Think of all the positive words and phrases used for a man who has many sexual partners – 'stud', 'Casanova', 'a bit of a lad' and so on. Then write down all the words used to describe a woman who has more than one sexual partner – 'slag', 'slut', 'trollop', 'local bike' and so on. Ask yourself the question, Why is this so?

Underpinning these descriptions of the same behaviours in men and in women are several persistent ideas: men have sexual urges that must be satisfied; men have less control over sexual urges than women do; women, especially wives, should be available for sexual intercourse when a man wants or demands it. Men who have more than one sexual partner are often admired by other men and some women, while women are denigrated. It is acceptable that a man leaves a trail of semen behind him, but unacceptable for the woman who behaves in a similar way. The presumption that men cannot control their sexual urges is insulting to those men who are perfectly able to control themselves, respect women and take responsibility for fathering a child.

Our next staging post is one of history's best-kept secrets, the Age of the Goddess and the rise of the phallus. Anthropological evidence is that in the Age of the Goddess women's fertility and sexuality were honoured. At that time, it is likely that gender characteristics reflected the reverence in which the female gods were held. However, over time, male gods replaced female gods, and kings reflected this shift of power in the replacement of queens. Men also appropriated the primary role in procreation, and the phallus became the organ of veneration.

CHAPTER FIVE:

THE DIVINE PHALLUS: THE SOURCE OF MALE POWER

Women have been the greatest race of underdogs the world has ever known. Recorded history is the history of only half of the human race – men. According to the historian Gibbon, in Ancient Rome 'History is little more than a register of the crimes, follies and misfortunes of men.'[1] One half of the human race has been excluded from history. A rereading of history demonstrates the 'violence and brutality of men's sustained attacks on the female sex, from wife-beating to witch hunting, from genital mutilation to murder'.[2] An objective look at history cannot deny this. One of the best-kept secrets in history is of the period when women assumed a special status due to the ability to produce new life, and the mystery of non-fatal yet incurable emissions of blood. This period (c.25,000 BC – 5000 BC) has been described by some commentators as 'The Age of the Goddess'.[3] This is not to say that there was a golden age when women were not subordinated by men, but archaeological evidence reveals a substantial period in pre- and early history when female gods were worshipped and revered.[4] Later, Father God religions dismissed accounts of the Age of the Goddess, or the Great Mother, as a myth or a cult. However, Sir Arthur Evans discovered the lost Minoan civilisation at the turn of the twentieth century, and the innumerable goddess figures he uncovered appear to represent the same Great Mother, who was worshipped under various names and titles and extended over a large part of Asia Minor and beyond.[5]

At the beginning of the twentieth century, modern scholarship accepted that the Great Goddess, the original 'Mother without a Spouse', prior to the emergence of Father God religions, was in full control of all the mythologies as a 'worldwide fact'. Scores of figurines of women have been found from Siberia to the Mediterranean. They include, for example, statuettes of pregnant women, and the Dolni Vestonice woman (c.26,400 BC), a small naked figurine with large, pendulous breasts and broad hips. These have been called mother goddesses, but there is little to explain women's relationship to men at the time. For example, from around 300 BC to 1200 BC Cretan culture favoured many depictions of women in seals, rings, bronzes, figurines and frescoes, but woman's role in Cretan society remains enigmatic.

Women's status in early communities may have been a consequence of the ability to bear children and to bleed regularly without dying; or because women gathered the bulk of food for the group. Male-centred anthropologists and historians promoted the idea that men were more necessary to the group because men did the hunting. Yet meat was only a small percentage of the diet. Recent studies of teeth of early humans show that their diet was mainly vegetarian. More recent scholarship has suggested that early groups operated as a community; hunting of large animals is more likely to have been done in a group, possibly driving sick or wounded animals to exhaustion or over a precipice.[6] The notion of woman sitting at home in the cave waiting for her man to return from hunting dragging a mammoth behind him is the stuff of myth.

It has been suggested by male historians and anthropologists that women's subordinate status was because women had an unequal share of the work of reproduction.[7] Women had to consent to domination in order to protect themselves and their children. Domination, however, was not a factor in every society. In some societies, men and women were equal. In fact, there is evidence that women's biological rites of passage, especially menstruation, were something to be envied and emulated.[8] Male-centred initiation rites suggest attempts to mimic women's biological rhythms. In the Aranda tribe of Australia, in order to be able to take the title 'possessor of a vulva', boy initiates undergo penis mutilation: a long, thin bone is inserted deep into the urethra and the penis cut with a small piece of flint. The penis is cut through the layers of flesh until the bone is reached and the penis opens up 'like a boiled frankfurter'. Regular reopening of the wound showed that the boy could now menstruate.[9] Many rites continue to survive in Stone Age cultures. 'In the beginning we had nothing, we took these things from women.'[10] Men gradually appropriated every area of women's perceived power: male gods replaced female gods; queens became the exception rather than the rule; religious meaning became the sole prerogative of men. Man was supreme.

> Man is active, full of movement, creative in politics, business and culture. The man shapes & moulds society and the world. Woman on the other hand is passive. She stays at home as is her nature. She is matter waiting to be formed by the active male principal. Man plays a major part in reproduction, the woman is merely the passive incubator of his seed . . . According to Aristotle, 'The male semen cooks and shapes the menstrual blood into a new human being.'[11]

As man appropriated the primary role in reproduction, he raised his status to 'co-creator' with God. The paradigm shift in thinking about who was responsible for the creation of new life was as significant as the Enlightenment, the Scientific Revolution and the Renaissance put together. Nevertheless, neither the significance of this nor the discovery of the ovum has yet to be fully discussed. This debate would challenge sexual differences and roles which have provided the norm for the past 6,000 years.

During the millennia immediately before the birth of Christ, all mythologies speak of the overthrow of the Great Mother Goddess. Whatever form it takes, the fundamental power shift from female to male is reflected in the emergence of patterns of dualisms. A key duality was that of sun and moon.

45

The divinity of the sun, lord of time and space was essentially masculine – the phallic sunbeams striking down on Mother Earth – a maleness impregnates the earth and causes the seeds to germinate.[12]

The male, represented by the sun, had positive characteristics of intellect, knowledge, light, growth, rebirth and renewal. The moon represented the dark, dreamy and watery characteristics of woman. This sun–moon dualism was applied to woman and man:

Whatever man is, woman is not, and with this imposition of the principal of sexual contrast comes the gradual definition of man as commanding all the human skills and abilities and woman as the half formed, half-baked opposite.[13]

The overthrow of the Great Mother did not happen overnight. Firstly, the Great Mother created the world; then she acquired a consort; the spouse/consort ruled equally with her; then he managed to rule without her.[14] The takeover of birth was the first step in the ultimate total domination of women. Man now considered himself to be the initiator of new life – a creator, ruler of the universe.

The phallus arose as the symbol of man's 'godlike' status; a handy symbol that he proudly carried around every day. 'His was the sacred organ of generation, the phallus, the source of all that lived.'[15] The male organ, the phallus, became the symbol and source of male power.

And what better weapon of dominance was there to hand but the phallus . . . in its fragile human form, prey to unbidden arousal, stubborn refusal and unpredictable deflation it could not compete with woman's unfailing power of birth . . . elevated above the reality into a symbol, transformed into 'phallus' and enshrined into materials such as metal and stone it would do very well.[16]

There is strong archaeological evidence to support the power of the phallus and phallus worship.[17] In Italy the god Phallus was part of the family. In India, the phallus, known as the 'celestial rod' of the god Shiva, reached from earth to heaven. The penis became the 'divine penis', the 'Phallus Lord'. Golden balls, orbs, swords and maces adorned monuments as symbols of masculinity and power. In Greece, instead of a corner shop, phallus pillars were erected on every street corner. By the third century BC an avenue of phalluses supported by huge testicles were built in Delos Pompeii; and the phallus god, Priapus, was worshipped. In Dorset, England, at Cerne Abbas, a giant figure 180 feet tall with a chest-high erection has been variously described as the Roman god Hercules or an early Saxon king. It is clear that whoever he was his enormous penis was a substantial symbol of male power.[18]

CHAPTER SIX:

WOMEN: FROM PRIESTS TO MERE OBSERVERS IN THE EARLY CHRISTIAN CHURCH

It is difficult to deduce with absolute certainty the role of women in prehistory; or the origins of their subordination to men. However, what we shall uncover suggests that regardless of when men began to subordinate women, at the root of this subordination is a presumed superiority supported by the beliefs and fantasies surrounding semen. Eventually, following the decline of the female gods, the one God who emerged in monotheistic religion assumed a higher status than the contemporary pagan collection of gods. The rise of monotheistic religion was accompanied by the rise of a clerical caste and a male hierarchy. Early Christians accepted the monotheism of Judaism and eventually the early Christian Church developed its own clerical caste. Nevertheless, this evolution was not simple or painless.

In spite of patriarchal attitudes among early Christian groups, the existence and development of the early Church depended on wealthy, influential women. Certainly, women were of service to the emerging Church; these women became effective protectors of the new churches around Palestine and Syria. Marcia, the concubine of the Emperor Commodus, obtained a letter granting freedom for martyrs in Sardinia. As late as the end of the third century AD, the mother of John Chrysostom (347–407), Olympias, spent twenty years supporting the Church at Constantinople.[1] However, in Judaism and in some pagan cultures the idea of the equality of women continued to be unacceptable. Women in Jewish communities were excluded from actively participating in public worship, in education and in social and political life outside the family.[2] Nevertheless, in its earliest years the Christian Church was remarkable in its openness to women.[3] It is evident in the discourses of the early Church that women played a prominent role in the developing Church. Ten to twenty years after the death of the founder women held positions of leadership in local Christian groups, acting as prophets, teachers and evangelists. Marcion (140–80) appointed women as priests and bishops; and women were accepted as leaders of Christian communities, performing all that would later be the sole prerogative of the male clergy.[4]

It may have been that the measure of equality which influential women were beginning to enjoy in surrounding societies had a resonance within the early Church. In Egypt, women had attained an advanced state of emancipation. In Rome, patriarchal forms of marriage were giving way to a new legal form in which man and woman bound themselves in voluntary and mutual vows. By the second century, upper-class women were often living their own lives involved in philosophy, literature, medicine and mathematics, but it is unlikely that all women enjoyed such status.

The dilemma for men in the early Christian Orthodox Church was how to accommodate women yet at the same time exclude them. The patriarchal belief that woman was an anomaly, different from men, provided for a limited number of responses (indifference, opportunism, exclusion and accommodation).[5] The Church could not afford to be indifferent to women as its very survival depended on them. As it could not be seen to be opportunistic, the rhetoric of women's accommodation became that of 'service', firstly to men and subsequently to the Church. Thus, the early Church reconciled the rhetoric of exclusion with social processes of accommodation.

An examination of the discourses of the early Christian Church reveals that early Christians were not an homogenous group, but made up of competing factions. The 'official' picture of the early Church is of a Christian community where possessions were shared; a single teaching was preached; and all believers worshipped together under the authority of the apostles. It was only after that 'golden age' that heresy and conflict emerged.[6] However, the discovery at Nag Hammadi, in 1945, of texts from the early Christian era reveals not one discourse, but several competing discourses among early Christian groups. Dissent amongst early Christian communities focused on two related issues: the nature of God and the power and authority of the clergy.[7] These early texts also reveal the centrality of assumptions of male superiority in orthodox discourse. The religious debates about the nature of God simultaneously bear social and political implications crucial to the development of Christianity; the rise of the clerical caste; and religious, social and political organisation.

The various Christian groups divided into either orthodox or Gnostic groups. In its simplest form, many Gnostic Christian groups correlated their description of God in both masculine and feminine terms. Most refer to the Creation account of Genesis 1, which suggests an equal or androgynous human Creation. Gnostic Christians often took the principle of equality between men and women into the social and political structures of their communities. Many Gnostic Christians talked of women as equal with men. On the other hand, the group who claimed primary legitimacy (which later became known as the orthodox Church) described God in exclusively masculine terms, and typically referred to Genesis 2 to describe how Eve was created for man and for his fulfilment. By the late second century, orthodox Christians had come to accept the domination of women by men as the divinely ordained order for the Church, in the social and political worlds, and in the family. The orthodox male God ensured the development of sex-specific solidarity structures, rites and rituals, from which women were excluded on the grounds of sex alone.

When Gnostic and orthodox Christians discussed the nature of God, they were at the same time debating the issue of spiritual authority. A male God gave religious legitimacy to male supremacy and male domination in the Church. Male supremacy, linked to the doctrine of the bodily Resurrection, established the initial framework for clerical authority. The risen Jesus gave Peter all authority on earth. In the absence of historical evidence for this, authority adherents must believe this to be the truth; to receive a share in this authority, bishops and priests must be able to trace their orders back to Peter. Even today the Pope traces his authority, and the primacy he claims over the rest, to Peter himself, 'the first of the apostles' since he was the 'first witness' of the Resurrection. The Gnostic Christians insisted the Resurrection was symbolic of a new experience of Christ's presence in one's life, which relied on an individual relationship with God, not necessarily mediated by the priesthood. Many Gnostic groups tended to regard all doctrines only as speculations or approaches to the truth.[8] Ultimately, orthodox Christians came to identify their own doctrines as the only 'truth' and awarded their leaders the right to interpret religious meaning for all Christian groups, and rejected all other discourses as heretical.

The orthodox insistence on 'one [male] God' simultaneously validated the system of governance in which the Church is ruled by 'one bishop' as monarch ('sole ruler') of the Church. The orthodox description of God (as, for example, Father Almighty) serves to define who is included in, and who is excluded from, participation in the power of priests and bishops.[9] The power of the male clergy was reinforced as obedience to God, which became synonymous with obedience to bishops, priests and deacons.

Whosoever refuses to bow the neck and obey Church leaders is guilty of subordination against the divine master himself.[10]

The initial equality enjoyed by women in the Church was lost, as the male God validated a system of governance which excluded women. The male God and a heavenly hierarchy validated the hierarchical, male-dominated clerical structure, which emerged in the early Church. The male God provided legitimacy for patriarchy within the orthodox Church. Patriarchal monotheisms do not merely imply female inferiority; they demand it. Man is made in the image of God; woman is not.

At this point, it should be noted that monotheism is not merely a religion; it is a relation of power. Any monotheistic religion contains notions of primacy and supremacy. In patriarchal religions, the concept of a relationship between God and man is exemplified in the belief that God created man in his own image; hence, God is reflected in every human patriarch. 'One God' has primacy over all others and adherents are supreme over non-believers. Monotheism is not exclusive to Christianity. The belief in the 'one God' is common to the major world religions of Judaism, Islam and Christianity. All of these monotheistic religions have assumed a duty to impose their beliefs on others. Jews persecuted other tribes whose idols challenged the 'one God', Christians persecuted Jews and Muslims, and Islam warred on Jews and Christians alike. Monotheism as a power relation inevitably creates a hierarchy of one God over all others, of stronger over weaker, of believer over unbeliever. Consequently, monotheism sets up some men to be the enemies of other men.

Elaine Pagels (1990) suggests that key factors in the success of the orthodox discourse were its claim to 'truth'; the simplicity of its recruitment by eliminating qualitative criteria for membership; and its appeal to existing patriarchal attitudes. By AD 200 both Gnostic and orthodox Christians claimed to represent the 'truth'. Gnosticism was for some regions 'Christianity' and they looked with scorn on the orthodox, labelling them as unbelievers. In the *Apocalypse of Peter*, orthodox Christians are the ones 'who oppose the truth and are messengers of error'.[11] The author accuses the orthodox Church of blind arrogance in claiming exclusive legitimacy.[12] In the text the *Authoritative Teaching*, they are 'dealers in bodies'(worse than Pagans with no excuse for their error).[13] The orthodox identified their doctrines as the truth – the only legitimate truth. By the end of AD 200 orthodox Christianity had become an institution headed by a three-rank hierarchy of bishops, priests and deacons. The leaders of the orthodox Church understood themselves to be the guardians of the only 'true faith'.[14]

In the orthodox Church, equal participation by women implicitly challenged assumptions of male superiority, hence male power. Orthodox reaction was to remind the Christian community of the divinely ordained order in which man was superior to woman and must control her. Paul, the apostle to the Gentiles, strongly influenced by Hebrew beliefs about man and woman, argued that as God has authority over Christ, so man has authority over woman. Confirming the stereotypical gender roles of patriarchy, the pseudo-Pauline letter of Timothy to Titus demonstrates women's role. Elderly widows were to be

> teachers of good things, that they may teach the young women to be sober, to love their husbands, to love their children, to be discreet, chaste, keepers at home, good, obedient to their own husbands, that the word of God might not be blasphemed.[15]

By the end of the second century AD, the majority of Christian churches opposed the move towards equality. The orthodox discourse was accepted as 'truth'. The orthodox community had accepted the domination of men over women, as the divinely ordained order, in both the family and in social life. Timothy's letter was endorsed as canonical. This letter demonstrates the anti-feminist element in Paul's views.

> Let a woman learn silence with all submissiveness. I permit no woman to teach or to have authority over men: she is to keep silent.

Paul's letter to the Colossians orders women to be subject in everything to their husbands.[16]

The orthodox Church, which adopted the synagogue custom of segregating women and men at worship, condemned levels of equality enjoyed by women in the other Christian Churches. By the end of the second century women's participation in worship was explicitly condemned; groups in which women continued on to leadership were branded as heretical.[17]

These heretical women, how audacious they are! They have no modesty; they are bold enough to teach, to engage in argument, to exact exorcisms, to undertake cures, and, it may be, even to baptize! . . . It is not permitted for a woman to speak in church, nor is it permitted for her to teach, nor to baptize, nor to offer [the Eucharist] nor to claim for herself a share in any masculine function, not to mention any priestly office.[18]

Throughout the first three centuries, it is evident that the discourse was becoming one of control. Repressive measures regulated what a woman should wear, how she should do her hair, even when she should wash. The orthodox Clement of Alexandria (c.180) laid down strict dress codes for women.

Women should be completely veiled, except when they are in the house. Veiling their faces ensures that they will lure no one into sin. For this is the will of Logos that it befits them to be veiled in prayer . . . the very consciousness of their own nature must evoke feelings of shame.[19]

Chrysostom bade women to 'be veiled not only at the time of prayer but continuously'.[20] The length of a woman's hair signified her 'natural' subjection to the male.[21] Control of women extended to personal hygiene. Women were warned against frequent washing.

Furthermore she [woman] should not wash all too frequently, not in the afternoon, nor every day. Let the tenth hour be assigned to her as the right time for bathing.[22]

Women were firmly placed in the private realm by Clement of Alexandria.

[Women] should be made to practice spinning wool and weaving, and helping with the baking of bread, when necessary. Women should also fetch from the pantry the things we need.[23]

It is noteworthy that early Christian texts did contain the names of women who were influential in the Church, but women were gradually removed from the public worship and from sacred texts. For example, in Romans 16:7 'Junia' has undergone a sex change and been renamed 'Junias'. Churchmen appropriated the work done by women in the early Church. Women's social and religious activities became increasingly controlled by Church Fathers.

By the third century, orthodox Christianity became the established religion of Imperial Rome. A monotheistic patriarchal religion swept across Europe together with Imperial Roman armies. As the established religion of Imperial Rome, the inferior position of women was assured in both Church and state. As the patriarchal Church was absorbed into Imperial Roman organisation the state gradually became the guarantor of patriarchal power. Constantine the Great (d.337) had a tremendous influence on the development of orthodox Christianity. Constantine was more concerned with state power than with religion when he adopted Christianity. He used Christianity as a way to unite the Empire. Despite popular belief, Constantine did not convert to Christianity until his deathbed; that is, he did not adopt and follow Christ, but adhered instead to the warrior God of the Old Testament. This was a significant deviation, for in so doing Constantine transformed Christianity into something completely different and assured the success of the patriarchal Church.[24] In this reversal, Christ, as the champion of the poor and oppressed, had no place in the Church of Imperial Rome. Constantine was concerned to provide absolute legitimation for his own values, and for all sovereigns to come. As emperor, he was declared as the manifestation of God on earth.

Once the orthodox Christian Church was adopted as the religion of Imperial Rome, it began to organise on an Imperial Roman model or organisation. It replicated the symbols of the Roman state. Eventually, the Bishop of Rome was given the Lateran Palace, and bishops became 'princes of the Church'. The 'princes of the Church' began to exercise dominion over administrative districts parallel to civil administrative districts of the Roman Empire. With the military might of Imperial Rome behind it, orthodox Christians were able to enforce their beliefs on the rest of the Christian communities. Patriarchal attitudes together with the power of the clergy led to a consolidation of male domination in the orthodox Christian Church. All those who refused to conform to orthodoxy were condemned as heretics. At the Council of Nicaea (325) Constantine took a leading role in rejecting as heretical all discourses other than those of orthodox Christianity. Control of other Christian sects was almost total as penalties for 'heresy' escalated. Every trace of heretical blasphemy was destroyed, or so it was thought, until the twentieth century and the discovery of the Gnostic gospels at Nag Hammadi.

Orthodox sexual theology developed over several centuries and depends on the 'truth' of male superiority for its legitimacy. The most significant development of sexual theology came with three 'Fathers of the Church' – Augustine, Albert and Aquinas. These men provided the foundations of a Christian sexual theology which was not displaced even by the great schism that was the Reformation in the sixteenth century, and which continues to underpin orthodox [Catholic] sexual theology in the twenty-first century. We continue to follow our trail of semen with Augustine, followed by Albert and, finally, Aquinas.

CHAPTER SEVEN:

SEMEN AND THE FOUNDATIONS OF SEXUAL THEOLOGY

The trail of semen can be followed from circa AD 300 through to the twenty-first century. However, the foundational beliefs that informed Christian doctrine were laid down by AD 1300. An examination of the writings of three important theologians – Augustine, Albert and Aquinas – reveals what these 'Fathers of the Church' believed about woman, man and semen. They supported and justified the idea of man's superiority and the inferiority of woman, and provided justification for the continued subjection and objectification of women for the next 1,000 years. Their ideas became an integral part of European thought, as orthodox Christianity became the chosen religion of Imperial Rome. The organisation of the orthodox Church was a key factor in the promulgation of these ideas throughout Europe. Church organisation mirrored that of the Roman state, and bishops as 'princes of the Church' became powerful.

Augustine not only identified woman as the site and cause of sin, but located original sin in the genitals. He also linked sexual renunciation (continence) with access to the 'truth'. Albert continued the fear of women and sexuality, and illustrated his misogyny through his slanderous comments about women. Aquinas elevated semen to a 'divine liquid'. Semen, now raised to the 'divine', led to the belief that priests who were celibate and retained their semen became 'angelic' with exclusive access to 'truth'. These theologians integrated ancient 'truths' about semen and about women into their theology; in so doing they cemented patriarchal beliefs about man and about woman into the sexual theology of the orthodox Christian Church and laid the foundations of a sexual theology that depends for its legitimacy on the fantasies surrounding semen.

In order to understand how celibates became 'angelic', and how semen became a 'divine liquid' we have to examine what these theologians presented as 'truth'. We shall begin with Augustine, whose ideas provided the foundations of Christian sexual theology, upon which Albert and Aquinas later built their 'truths'. Earlier we noted the importance of the Creation story, and its role in a presumption of male superiority and the need to control women. Augustine added a few details to the story of the Garden of Eden, which led to the notion of 'original sin'. He linked this 'original sin' to sexual intercourse. Eve was naturally cast as the villain, who tempted a weak-willed Adam to have sex.

Later, as we examine the writings of Albert, there is strong evidence that he confirmed woman as a temptress and untrustworthy; and intensified the fear and hatred of women in the Christian world. Albert, dubbed by the theologian Uta Ranke-Heinemann as the patron saint of rapists, was convinced that if a woman said no she really meant yes.

Finally, Aquinas, coached by Albert, found that recently rediscovered works by the Greek philosophers confirmed all that was believed about man and woman. He took these ideas from the ancient world as 'evidence' for the superiority of man, the inferiority of woman and the beliefs concerning semen. These ideas, however, were not 'evidence' of patriarchal beliefs, but were confirmation of the continuity and persistence of the myths and fantasies surrounding semen, from the ancient world to the Middle Ages. These theologians gave these myths and fantasies new life and impetus.

By the end of the Middle Ages, the superiority of man, the elevation of the male celibate and the role of semen were cemented into Christian thought and practice. The male celibate had exclusive access to 'truth'; man together with God was the co-creator of new life; semen as the primary life source was to be protected. Woman was confirmed merely as the incubator for man's seed. Control over women and children was absolute and stereotypical images of women persisted. Women had less and less control over their own bodies and contraception was conflated to murder. Divorce for a woman was out of the question as woman's mental incapacity was affirmed as the reason to keep a woman under the control of a man.

Augustine Aurelius was born in Algeria to a pagan father and a Christian mother. As a young man, Augustine lived a hedonistic lifestyle. He had a long-term affair with a woman, but abandoned her, even though they had a child, because she was not of his social class. Augustine's mother Monica (later St Monica) found a suitable bride for him, but he had to wait for two years before he could wed her; so he took another mistress. Augustine became involved in the Manichean religion, which saw Creation as flawed, containing within it both good and evil. Eventually, at the age of forty-two, Augustine converted to Christianity. He was baptised in AD 387. His works influenced later Church theologians, especially Aquinas. He is sometimes called the 'Father of Roman Catholicism', which was *the* Christian Church until the great schism that was the Protestant Reformation.

By the time of Augustine, sexual theology established that the body itself was the site of sin. Augustine's contribution to the discourse was to identify more precisely the site of sin, namely the genitals in the act of intercourse. The focus for Augustine at this point is his doctrine of original sin, which institutionalised woman as the entry point of evil into the world. He argued that all sin originated with the 'original' sin, which had come from the sexual act. His evidence for the assumption that original sin had come from the genitals was that after Adam and Eve had disobeyed God 'They were ashamed and covered their sexual parts with fig leaves.' Augustine concluded, 'This is where it [original sin] comes from.'[1] It was through sexual intercourse that original sin was passed from generation to generation. Eve, in the place of all women, had tempted Adam to sin. Sin entered the world via a woman. Man would not have sinned if woman had not tempted him. Woman was therefore the site and cause of sin. It followed that all women posed a threat to all men.

Crucial factors in Augustine's formulation of his doctrine of original sin were patriarchal beliefs, a fear of women and sexuality, and Manichean pessimism. Prejudicial notions about women and their bodies are evident as Eve, not Adam, was identified as the cause of sin in the world.[2] Woman's body, not man's body, is the site of sin. In his concern to ascertain whether Adam and Eve had sexual intercourse, he reveals a link with the beliefs of the wider world.

> I do not see what sort of help woman was created to provide men with, if one excludes the purpose of procreation . . . what other help could she be?[3]

In other words, woman is only good for sex. Augustine was convinced that had Eve not tempted Adam to sin, the human race would have remained in a state of prelapsarian purity.

This doctrine of original sin plays a significant part in the assumption that the continent male priest has privileged access to truth. Augustine argued that sexual intercourse would not have been necessary in the Garden of Eden (presumably, some sort of paradisiacal cloning would have occurred); it was only after Eve had tempted Adam to sexual intercourse that an angelic state of purity was compromised. The continent male was the closest one could get to the previous state of angelic purity.[4] As such, the continent male who resisted temptation and retained his semen was spiritually elevated above all other believers. The elevated state of purity was presumed to provide access to 'truth', which was denied to those who engaged in sexual activity. The angelic state of the continent male was confirmed by Aquinas.[5] The presumed access to a higher state of being later supported the institution of celibacy. Augustine's conclusion that original sin came from sexual intercourse ensured that sexual activity and sin would have the highest profile in Christian theology. The identification of woman as the site and cause of sin ensured that women, sexuality and sin would be inextricably bound together; and the doctrine of original sin became a cornerstone of Christian objective 'truth'. Implicit in this doctrine are the association of woman with nature, physicality and evil; and the elevation of the continent male, which associated men with spirituality.

The writings of Augustine supported patriarchy in the Church, in society and in the family through the paterfamilias (the head of a Roman family – the oldest living male in a household). The inferior status of woman confirmed her role as that of 'service' to men and to the Church. A woman was subject to her husband, his property, his slave. Augustine used his mother, Monica, to remind women that their role in life was to serve men. He explained:

> When she [Monica] reached marriageable age she was given to a husband whom she served as master . . . They [wives] had all heard, she said, the marriage contract read out to them and from that day they ought to regard it as a legal instrument by which they were made servants; so they should remember their station and not set themselves up against their masters.[6]

Despite her husband's infidelities, Monica avoided quarrels by never complaining.

It is evident from Augustine's discourse that his sexual theology was strongly influenced by the patriarchal beliefs and assumptions of the wider world. Augustine's theology was rooted in biologically determined theories about woman and man. His doctrine of original sin was influenced by his beliefs in the inferiority of woman together with a fear of women and sexuality. The notion of an original sin linked to sexual intercourse had a significant impact on the discourse on women and on the attitudes of continent males regarding women. This doctrine supported and sustained beliefs of the wider world concerning the dangerousness of women, sexual activity and pollution. Women's bodies were the site of sin, and sexual intercourse was the expression of sin; women, sex and sin were intertwined. Continent males feared and avoided women, who were seen as a threat to their sanctity. Women's only acceptable role was to serve men and provide the means of procreation.

We pause for a moment to examine the notion of original sin and its implications. Original sin is a fundamental doctrine in Christianity. All people are presumed to be born with original sin. Unless this sin is removed by Christian baptism, the soul is condemned to eternal damnation. Even when the sin is removed by baptism the sin 'weakens' the human person and hence explains their proclivity to sin. The presumed damnation of those who died with original sin on their souls gave 'permission' for the forced conversion of many non-Christians in the name of God.

There were a few practical problems to overcome; and the doctrine of original sin is a clear example of adjustments and increments to the original idea, which had not been fully thought through. One problem was that of what happened to unbaptised infants. Augustine insisted that all souls who had not had original sin removed by baptism would go to hell. However, some of his contemporaries did not agree with him. Bishop Julian of Eclanum, a Pelagian, disagreed with Augustine's damnation of unbaptised children and sharply attacked him.

> Augustine, you are far removed from religious feelings, from civilised thinking, indeed from healthy common sense, if you think that your God is capable of committing crimes against justice that are scarcely imaginable even for the barbarians.

Julian called Augustine's God 'a persecutor of infants, who throws babies into eternal fire'.[7] Julian was Bishop of Eclanum from 416. He was a married, educated priest whose wife was the daughter of the Bishop of Benevento. Julian opposed the sexual pessimism of Augustine and had a positive attitude towards sexual pleasure. It was one of the 'goods' of marriage. He defended the sexual urge,

> not as some outstandingly good thing, but as a drive in our bodies made by God – a drive which you claim has been put in us by the devil, making your whole doctrine stand or fall on the discreet behaviour that surrounds the sexual act.

Julian felt that the sexual urge was the same for Adam and Eve as it was for married couples. He felt that the sexual urge needed at times to be controlled, but could never be said to be 'fallen'. It was blameworthy only in its excesses.[8] Augustine rejected Julian's alternative view and, determined to discredit him, wrote unceasingly against him. Julian was eventually ousted from the Church as a heretic. Augustine held on to Manichean ideas of a permanent evil existing in human beings and remained a determining spiritual force in Christianity.[9]

Another problem to overcome was that of Mary, the mother of Jesus, who could not be born with original sin. The solution was to declare that Mary was a virgin, and was the only human being to have been born without original sin; hence, she could not pass this sin on to her child Jesus. There was also the question of who should be saved in childbirth if there was a choice between mother and child. In some Catholic countries, women still find that their lives can be sacrificed in order that the unborn child can be baptised. Doctrinally, it is more important that the child be baptised quickly before imminent death than that the mother be allowed to live after the death of an unbaptised child. It was not until the late twentieth century that it became acceptable for clinicians to make a choice between mother and baby, but only when both were in danger of dying. In a plain choice between mother and baby, the baby was to be saved. Celibates appealed to a woman's conscience when deciding whether to save herself or her unborn child, but the choice for many women could be much more complicated than that.

Despite the transmission of original sin from one generation to the next, the sexual act was necessary if the species was to survive. Augustine had to find a way to 'allow' sexual intercourse. He reasoned that man is 'naturally' inclined to lust because of original sin. Man needs to satisfy this urge to evil, but the power that was sex was not to be trusted to ordinary people; they must be guided. Sexual activity must be contained, and where better to contain it than in marriage? Augustine defined the three 'goods' of marriage as children, fidelity and indissolubility. Within these three goods, lust can be properly contained. In summary, men were doomed to sin, as a permanent evil existed in the human body – that of sexual desire and pleasure.[10] A pessimistic sexual morality permitted sexual intercourse only in marriage; and women were classified as stimulants, not partners. With Augustine the sexual act was to be mechanical, a call to procreation alone, reduced to an animalistic level with no personal component at all. Augustine decided that before the 'fall' of the human race, represented by Adam and Eve, the sexual urge had been aroused by the will alone, without the excitement of lust.[11] His horror of lust formed a firm foundation for future Christian understanding of sex.

The notion of fidelity in marriage focused on the woman. Augustine approved of polygamy, which he described as an 'unselfish act'. The approval of polygamy ignores the needs and dignity of women, reducing their role to the containment of male lust; and as baby-making machines.

> I rather approve using the fertility of many women for an unselfish purpose than using the flesh of a single woman for her own sake.[12]

Polygamy does not contradict the order of Creation, but polyandry does, because women are their husband's slaves.

> Now a slave never has several masters, but a master does have several slaves. Thus we have never heard that the holy women served several living husbands, but we do read that many holy women served one husband.[13]

Augustine was also concerned about the use of contraception. The rhythm method, by which sexual activity was restricted to those periods when a woman was unlikely to conceive, turned those who used it into 'adulterers' and 'whoremongers'.

> It turns away from what marriage is for. Husbands turn wives into shameful harlots and the marriage bedrooms into bordellos and fathers-in-law are pimps.[14]

As the clerical caste gradually tightened their hold over the sexual lives of the Christian faithful (through threats of excommunication and final damnation), another valuable weapon in the armoury of control of sexual activity was that of 'forbidden times'. Forbidden times were strengthened and extended by Augustine. Certain days of the week, the period after Confession and before receiving Communion, and longer periods such as the forty days of Lent, were gradually extended until they covered almost six months of a year. Over time, sex in 'forbidden times' became the explanation for all manner of sickness and malformations in the newborn child. Consequently, children and parents – in particular, the mother – were ostracised.

Augustine, therefore, laid the basis for Christian sexual theology. The cornerstone of Augustine's theology is that of original sin. He affirmed male superiority, ensured the subordinate position of women, laid the blame for evil in the world at the feet of woman the temptress, strengthened the weapon of 'forbidden times' and increased the power of the clerical caste.

The discourse of Albert, however, reflected the prejudicial notions about women in a patriarchal Church and a patriarchal world. Albert was a misogynist and many of his ideas about women continue into the twenty-first century. This part of the trail of semen is supplemented by several quotes given in full; these illustrate most clearly Albert's attitude towards women. Albert, later given the title 'the Great', was a thirteenth-century German Dominican. He was influenced by Aristotelian philosophy, which had reached Europe through the Arab world. Despite Albert's reputation as a searcher for the truth, it is evident that he was influenced by patriarchal gender stereotypes. Albert clearly believed that women were less qualified than men for moral behaviour and were liars, untrustworthy and sly. Also evident in his discourse is a continuity of ideas from the ancient world which negatively affected women.

Woman is a misbegotten man and has a faulty and defective nature . . . she is unsure of herself. What she cannot get she seeks to obtain through lying and diabolical deceptions . . . one must be on one's guard with a woman as if she were a poisonous snake and the horned devil . . . woman is not cleverer but slyer, more cunning than man. Cleverness sounds like something good, slyness sounds like something evil. Thus in evil and perverse doings woman is cleverer that is, slyer than man, her feelings drive women towards evil, just as reason impels man toward good.[15]

As mentioned earlier, the theologian Uta Ranke-Heinemann gave Albert the title of patron saint of rapists; Albert stated very clearly that when women say no they really mean yes. This idea continues in the twenty-first century as an excuse for rape.

As I heard in the confessional in Cologne, delicate wooers seduce women with careful touches. The more these women seem to reject them, the more they really long for them and resolve to consent to them. But in order to appear chaste, they act as if they disapprove of such things.[16]

The status of semen was reinforced with the introduction by Albert of Aristotelian philosophy into Christian theology. Greek philosophy found a convenient resting place in Christian sexual theology. The rediscovery of Greek writings which had been preserved in the Arab world confirmed for Albert, and later Aquinas, that their beliefs about women were 'proven' by these ancient texts. Albert's remarks about women also demonstrate most clearly the continuity between the beliefs of the Greco-Roman world and the Christianity of the Middle Ages. Albert and his pupil Aquinas incorporated much of this 'new' thought into Church dogma. Aquinas would synthesise Greek 'wisdom' and Christian theology.

Thomas Aquinas was a priest and philosopher who influenced centuries of religious and academic thought. He worked to reconcile the rediscovered philosophies of Aristotle and Plato with Christian theology. He used Aristotelian arguments to 'prove' God's existence and the 'truth' of Christian beliefs.

> Aquinas . . . if he adopted and adapted a number of Aristotelian theories, [did so] not because they were Aristotle's nor yet because he thought them useful, but because he believed them to be true.[17]

The Church adopted his thinking, later called Thomism. He was canonised in 1323. In 1879, Pope Leo XII declared Aquinas's works 'the only true philosophy'.

With Aquinas, the prejudicial discourse about women is cemented into Christian theology in a practical way. Aquinas confirms the patriarchal construction of woman as mentally, physically and spiritually inferior to men; this supports and sustains the justification for male control over women and their bodies. Aquinas reflects almost exactly the ancient construction of woman as an inferior being. Man is the norm against which to measure woman. Reminiscent of ideas from the Greek texts, he notes that in unfavourable circumstances a woman – that is, a 'misbegotten' man – is born. Woman is 'a defect that does not correspond to nature's first intention' and 'originating in some defect'.[18] They [women] did not respond to 'nature's first intention', which aims for perfection, but to 'nature's second intention . . . decay, deformity and the weakness of age'.[19]

The only use Aquinas (as Augustine before him) can find for women in God's plan is that 'Woman is intended for procreation.' That exhausts her usefulness.[20] Aquinas confirmed that women were sexual objects to be used by men. Woman's primary function was that of a receptacle for semen and the nurture of the foetus.

Convinced of man's superiority, with his role as co-creator (with God) of new life, Aquinas focuses much attention on semen; and the fantasies surrounding semen reach new heights. Following the Greek philosophers and physicians, Aquinas recognises semen as the active element in procreation. He starts with the principle that every active element creates something like itself.

> The energy in semen aims of itself to produce something equally as perfect, namely another man.[21]

Aquinas describes semen as this 'divine liquid'.[22] (Implicit in this assumption is the further elevation of man – the possessor of semen – almost to the divine). As Aquinas elevated semen to the 'divine', he reinforced the idea of the inferiority of women; women were confirmed as mere vessels for the 'divine liquid'. Aquinas's concern about semen increased; the 'divine liquid' must be protected. Sexual activity became hedged in with rules and regulations, forbidden times and permissions for indulgence. Sexual activity must be contained if semen was to be protected.

With Aquinas, the links between ideas, discourse and practice are evident. His theology is one of the most significant staging posts on our trail of semen down through the ages, as semen is elevated to the 'divine'. For Aquinas, as for Augustine before him, the dilemma was that 'divine' semen must be protected, but at the same time it must also be used for procreation. He was aware that sexual intercourse between men and women could not be stopped entirely. He said that he had never met a husband who could claim that 'he had sexual relations only in the hope of conception'.[23] There is a certain refreshing honesty in those husbands who told Aquinas that they enjoyed sex. That some husbands admitted their failure to always think of procreation holds out some hope that some of the people remained reasonably sane, protecting themselves from the worst excesses of the celibate obsession with sex by ignoring them and their edicts.

How could semen be protected and at the same time be used in the sexual act? How could these two positions be reconciled? Following Augustine, Aquinas took a pragmatic approach and gave married couples 'excuses' for sexual intercourse. Sex was for procreation or the avoidance of (male) fornication. Aquinas was also concerned that some married couples may not have procreation in the forefront of their minds when indulging in sexual intercourse. In his concern to protect semen, Aquinas confined the sexual act outside forbidden times, forbidden couplings, forbidden reasons and forbidden practices. The concern to protect semen intruded into the bedrooms of married couples. The male celibates dictated how, when and why semen should be released into 'the vessel'. Semen must be delivered in a proper manner into the correct vessel, within the proscribed times and for the right reason. The correct vessel was the womb; the correct times were those decided by the clerical caste; the only correct coupling was husband and wife; the correct reason was to beget a child; the proper manner was the missionary position (Albert had told Aquinas that if a woman lay on top of a man the uterus was upside down so the semen would fall out.)[24] The 'natural' position was to have a woman on her back. Positions other than this 'missionary position' were considered most seriously sinful, as they were 'unnatural' forbidden practices. For so-called continent males, they appear to have had a surprising amount of knowledge about the sexual act and female anatomy.

The most heinous sins were reserved for those where semen was not delivered in the proper manner, to the correct vessel, and for the right reasons. Aquinas considered that vices worse than incest, rape and adultery were masturbation, bestiality, homosexuality, anal and oral intercourse and coitus interruptus.[25] Concern for semen overwhelmed any possible consideration for the 'vessel' – that is, woman. Woman was confirmed as an object to be used by men for the avoidance of fornication and for procreation. There was also a fear that some individuals may even indulge in sexual intercourse purely for pleasure. In addition, in order to restrict opportunities for men to seek forbidden pleasure elsewhere, a wife must always be open to her husband's advances so that he would not find release outside the marriage bed. Wives were to blame if men were not sexually satisfied at home. This idea also had a long shelf life.

In the overwhelming concern to protect semen, every act of sexual intercourse must be for procreation; coitus interruptus or contraception in any form was forbidden. In any act of intercourse, a woman must always be open to the reception of semen. By the fifteenth century, contraception had been inflated to murder.

> Those affected with this vice are murderers of human beings . . . truly murderers of children.[26]

Therefore, after the sin of murder, the sin of preventing generation came second. In the sixteenth century, Pope Sixtus V introduced the death penalty (for women) for contraception through potions. Justification for such a severe sanction was that reproduction must remain in the hands of men for:

> If women were to be allowed to prevent conception . . . this would be an astonishing abuse and great damage would be done to human reproduction.[27]

Evidently, women were not able to make independent decisions about contraception. Men must control a woman's fecundity.[28] Echoing the views of the Greek philosophers, Aquinas said that a woman needed a man to control her and spoke of woman as mentally defective.

> [Woman] has a defect in her reasoning ability, also evident in children and mentally ill persons.[29]

A woman needed a man to think for her, to guide her and to instruct the next generation. Consequently, Aquinas also dismissed the possibility of divorce because:

> Woman is in no way adequate to educate children...the father on account of his more perfect reason [can better] instruct the children

and

The woman needs the man not only for generating and educating children but also for her personal master [for the man] is of more perfect reason and stronger virtue.[30]

While there are continuities between Greek thought and the theology of Albert and Aquinas, there is a significant difference. In the Greco-Roman world the concern for semen was linked to the 'care of the self'.[31] The loss of 'vital spirit' or semen was linked to death, ill-health or becoming 'womanish'. The sex act was associated with the whole body coming together in one act. The genitals were afforded no special place, but performed together with the whole body; they were mere points of passage.[32] In Christianity, the unregulated ejaculation of semen became synonymous with sin and death of the soul. Christian sexual theology came to rest on the protection of semen and the control of genital sex. As it did so, the control of women and their bodies increased.

In describing woman as a 'misbegotten' man, Aquinas illustrates most clearly a direct continuity between the beliefs and assumptions of the Greek philosophers and the sexual theology of the Christian Church. The elevation of semen to the status of 'divine liquid' strengthened the imperative to protect semen. Unlawful emissions of semen were confirmed as sinful and sexual activity became hedged in with sanctions and prohibitions. Woman was confirmed as a mere vessel for man's 'seed' and penalties for women who practiced contraception escalated. It is evident that Christian sexual theology was influenced by the world from which it sprang.

The patriarchal discourse in the world in which Christianity took root was a discourse of biological determinism in which woman was constructed as man's inferior other. Patriarchal discourses led to discursive practices which subordinated women. We have seen that women were active in the early Church, but were gradually excluded from public participation. A male God justified religious, political and social arrangements that excluded women. A patriarchal discourse supported and sustained the rising power and authority of the clerical caste and supported their claim to define and explain truth. As the orthodox Church increased its sphere of influence, the bio-theology of orthodoxy became generally accepted as a 'divine truth' and all other discourses were denounced as heretical. The incorporation of Greek philosophy into Christian sexual theology is evidence of the absorption of beliefs from the ancient world concerning male superiority. These beliefs support and sustain patriarchy in the Christian Church.

Christian sexual theology is rooted in the fantasies surrounding semen, which emerge from the biological determinism of patriarchy. It follows that sexual theology is a theology of semen. As such, any challenge to the biological arguments for male superiority is a direct challenge to Christian sexual theology and to the structures and institutions that arise from that theology. We shall see in later chapters that, through sexual theology and the patriarchal state, notions of male superiority have persisted into the twenty-first century. The emphasis on sexual sins continues to be the hallmark of Catholic Christianity, which claims continuity with the early orthodox Church. In Catholic Christianity, a celibate hierarchy continues to attempt to control women and reproduction. But between the Middle Ages and the twenty-first century there have been significant changes in Europe, which have not only affected the claim by the male celibates to define and explain truth, but which have challenged the nature of truth itself. The Renaissance, the Reformation and the Scientific Revolution resulted in a new view of the world, which challenged traditional myths and 'truths'. It is to this staging post we now turn.

CHAPTER EIGHT:

INSTITUTIONAL CELIBACY: THE BACKBONE OF THE PATRIARCHAL CHURCH

At this stage on our journey, we consider the institution of celibacy and its role in maintaining male power in the orthodox Catholic Christian Church. Notions of purity and continence (perpetual sexual abstinence) are linked to a (presumed) privileged access to 'truth'. In the institution of celibacy, priests are expected to retain their semen. We shall also note that the requirement of sexual renunciation has not always been linked to priesthood; nor has continence and priesthood been a constant tradition in the Christian Churches. Why therefore should continence be required for priesthood? What is the function of continence, the practice of which has become institutionalised in celibacy? Whose interests does it serve? How is institutional celibacy connected to sexual theology? Does the presumed access to truth (which Augustine afforded to the male continent body) remain? If so, is it a presumption that extends to all celibates or only the few? How is institutional celibacy connected to patriarchy in the Church and in society? Does institutional celibacy contribute to the continued inferior position of women in the orthodox Christian Church? Is it a barrier to the priesthood for women? So many issues are linked to the institution of celibacy; therefore it is a legitimate avenue for examination.

Over the latter half of the twentieth century, the Christian Churches have been affected by the growth of materialism and secularisation in the Western world. A lack of male vocations together with an ageing clergy has affected almost all Christian denominations. Several Christian Churches accepted women to the priesthood or ministry as vocations from men all but dried up. The orthodox Catholic Christian Church continues to refuse women's ordination. In the Catholic Church, opposition to institutional celibacy remains a live issue, not least because over the last half of the twentieth century over 100,000 priests left the ministry.[1] It has been suggested that compulsory celibacy is a factor in this exodus.

An examination of the emergence of celibacy as a prerequisite for priesthood reveals that institutional celibacy was not always mandatory in the Church; neither was it a state of perpetual continence freely chosen. It emerged gradually over many centuries as a discipline imposed upon a reluctant priesthood. Indeed, in the early Church perpetual continence was not linked to priesthood. That there were married priests in the early Church is implicit in the ruling of the Council of Nicaea (AD 325) that there should be no marriage *after* the reception of a high office in the Church. Celibacy as a requisite for priesthood only emerged after centuries of resistance.[2]

During this period, it can be shown that priests were able to marry and have children. So, what was the imperative to enforce the celibate state on priests? It appears that much of the pressure to conform was economic. Pope Agapitus (535–36) tightened the knot between celibate practice and control of material possessions by opposing the practice of popes to choose their own successors. During the reign of Pope Gregory the Great, the Council of Seville (592) declared the sons of priests to be illegitimate; thereby ensuring that Church property would remain within the Church. It was evident that priests continued to marry for the next several centuries; Benedict VIII (1012–24) was only able to prohibit marriage and concubinage among the clergy with the permission of Henry II of Bamberg. The institutionalisation of celibacy was a long, slow, painful process.

Eventually, a male celibate hierarchy emerged in which celibacy became the requirement for all those who would hold power and authority in the Church. A minority of celibates took to themselves the authority to define and explain 'truth', and to institutionalise celibacy. In 1139 at the Second Lateran Council, those celibates who held power and authority declared all marriages of priests null and void, and demanded that existing marriages be severed before a man could be ordained to priesthood.[3] This was the first time that continence and celibacy were identified as the same thing. Celibacy no longer meant non-marriage, but a rejection of sexual activity in all its forms.

This sexual shift transferred all power and authority in the hierarchal, orthodox Christian Church into the hands of a few male celibates. Institutional celibacy was the final moulding of the power of a sacerdotal caste system. Not all continent celibates were permitted to define 'truth'. An elite group of celibates now held power and authority in the Church and imposed their 'truths' on the majority of priests and the faithful. It remains a clear example of how, in patriarchal systems and organisations, some powerful men control other men as well as all women and children. A barrier was set up between the hierarchy and the rest of the clergy; between the clergy and the people,[4] but especially between the clergy and women.

On our trail of semen, the institution of celibacy is a critical staging post. The notion of access to 'truth' by the continent male celibate is presumed through the retention of semen. If we glance back to a previous staging post, we can see links made between sexual activity and sin; and continence linked to sanctity and a return to prelapsarian purity. But if the state of continence alone was the requirement for a return to prelapsarian purity, surely every continent woman or man would achieve this purity and access to 'truth' in the same way as the celibate male priest. The vital difference between male and female continence is the underpinning belief in the superiority of the male. As we have seen, this presumption of superiority depends for its legitimacy on the fantasies surrounding semen. It is the possession and retention of semen that elevates the male celibate to a prelapsarian purity and privileged access to 'truth'. Therefore, any challenge to traditional beliefs about male superiority and the status of semen is a challenge to the power of the male celibate hierarchy and the priestly caste.

What was happening to the wives of priests during the period when celibacy was becoming codified? The negative view of women is evident in the manner in which they were treated; women, of less value than men, were objects to be used and then discarded. The Synod of Pavia (1022) decreed that children of priests' wives and concubines would become serfs. In 1081, the Synod of Melfi declared that the women and wives of clergy were to be taken as slaves, and their children declared illegitimate; a witch-hunt for clergy wives and women was the result. Not content with condemning women and their children to slavery, the Synods of Valladolid (1322), Valencia (1388), Cologne (1415) and Paris (1429) declared that women who had sexual relations with a priest would be denied a Christian burial. At this time, and for many following centuries, this was a frightening prospect for a believer, for to die and be buried without the rites of the Church was to be condemned to hell for all eternity.

With marriages forbidden, the fourteenth and fifteenth centuries saw a rise in concubinage, which was not restricted to the lower ranks of the clergy. Even the popes had sexual relations with women. Clement VI (1342–52), was accused by his contemporaries of illicit sexual relations. John XXII (1410–15) was said to have seduced around 200 women during his five-year reign. Pius II (1458–64) and Innocent VII (1484–92) left a trail of illegitimate children fathered prior to their ordinations.[5] No doubt their access to a prelapsarian purity and access to 'truth' was delayed until after their ordinations. The bitter irony was that while the male half of these liaisons moved upward in power and esteem in the Church, the women who were involved were increasingly persecuted.[6]

It is hard to overestimate the importance of anti-feminism in the formation of the celibate consciousness and priestly development over two centuries, when the discipline of celibacy was being codified. In Church tradition, the only good woman is silent, sexless and subservient. Church documents of the time describe the male virgin as 'one not *defiled* by woman'; and the male celibate must for ever be on his guard against woman as she is a threat to his purity.[7] Institutional celibacy is not only linked to the oppression of women in the Church, it is the backbone of a patriarchal Church.

The schism in Western Christianity known as the Reformation (c.1517–1648) challenged the power of the celibate priestly caste. Access to the Bible through the development of the printing press meant that literate lay people could read and interpret the word of God. The priestly role as a necessary intermediary between the people and God was undermined. Christendom split into several 'Churches' with differing ideas about salvation. What remained the same in the majority of these Churches was the notion of male superiority. As we shall see in the next chapter, there was no Reformation for women or for semen.

CHAPTER NINE:

THE PROTESTANT REFORMATION: NO REFORMATION FOR SEMEN

One of the greatest challenges to the power of the celibate priestly caste came with the schism in Western Christianity known as the Reformation. Up until this time, the Western Church was one Church, led by the Bishop of Rome, which conformed to the orthodox view of Christianity. That is not to say that there was no difference of opinion in the Church; there had always been dissenters from the orthodox view. Most dissenters were condemned as heretics or absorbed into the family of the Church through initiating a range of holy orders requiring different disciplines and practices. But change was inevitable, as the period from the fourteenth century to the seventeenth century saw major shifts in European thought. Prior to the Reformation, the Age of Reason had been a feature of the sixteenth century. The new emphasis on reason and scientific analysis led to revolutions in science, philosophy, society and politics. These revolutions challenged long-held beliefs and traditions.

Consequently, many institutions and traditional lines of authority were undermined. These challenges affected the Christian Church. A new view of the world undermined the entire set of presuppositions (rooted in biological determinism) that underpinned philosophical inquiry and sexual theology. This new way of understanding and explaining the world developed its own new constructs; 'truths' depended on reason and scientific enquiry rather than on myths, magic or faith.

The new ideas spread quickly around Europe due in part to the increase in literacy and developments in papermaking and printing techniques. There was a certain inevitability of a revolution of ideas, which culminated in France, leading to the destruction of the traditional hierarchical, political and social orders of the monarchy and the Catholic Church. These forms of power and authority were replaced by political and social organisation informed by ideals of freedom and equality. France based its new order on '*Liberté, égalité, fraternité*'. The Scientific Revolution, the Enlightenment and the Reformation challenged not only previously held 'truths', but the basis of Christian sexual theology itself.

During the Reformation, the notion of individual access to truth and to God was the beginning of the end for the celibate's privileged access to 'truth'; and the power of the clergy was undermined. The interpretation of the Bible had been the prerogative of the clerical caste, but people were beginning to interpret the Bible for themselves. The orthodox interpretations of the Bible stories were under threat. The presumed 'angelic' prelapsarian state of the continent male and his access to 'truth' depended upon the 'truth' of the Creation story, and a biologically determined sexual theology. Aware of the challenge to the position of the celibate male, the Catholic Christian Church reacted to the new ideas with a Counter-Reformation.

The Counter-Reformation began with the Council of Trent (1547). A strict Catholic orthodoxy, based on the philosophy of the High Scholastics in the Middle Ages, was imposed. It was a reinforcement of the doctrines of Augustine and Aquinas. No revision of doctrine emerged. Orthodox truth was reaffirmed as absolute. Sexual theology remained intact. There was no reformation for semen. A pre-Enlightenment and pre-Reformation world view permeated doctrine and remained embedded in the everyday experience of priesthood and the laity.

The Council of Trent heralded the beginning of the celibate retreat from the world. Gradually, the Catholic Christian Church became a fortress within which it was safe from the contamination of the world. The walls of the fortress were strengthened when Darwin published his *Origin of Species* in 1859. Inside the fortress, more effective control of the sexual behaviour of priests was possible as priests were 'formed' within a total institution that had rejected the world. Traditional ideas about women as 'temptresses' continued. Consequently, at the beginning of the twentieth century, orthodox Catholic priests formed within a total institution were influenced by an anti-modernism mentality and a sexual theology that condemned woman as the site and source of sin. Notions of 'impurity' continued to be reflected in women's access to sacred spaces and 'churching' (cleansing) following childbirth.

It was during these years that the institution of celibacy finally took a firm hold. Almost total control of ministerial conduct was achieved through the control of information and of sexual behaviour. Well into the twentieth century, the Catholic laity and their priests were expected to abide by the decisions of the Pope. The Pope and a small group of other celibates continued in their attempt to control the sexual lives of men, women and priests. Celibate priests continued to be considered holier than the laity, due to their state of continence. The powerful, overriding explanation for celibacy – that of the spiritual superiority of the male celibate – was reinforced. The myths surrounding semen and the link between sanctity and access to truth remained in place. The patriarchal Church with its belief in male superiority remained intact. A fatally flawed sexual theology, which depends upon the superiority of the male and the fantasies surrounding semen, continued to underpin sexual theology within the 'Fortress Church'.

Following the Reformation the hegemony of Christendom was shattered. The presumed prerogative of the celibate male to define and interpret truth was challenged and undermined. Most new Christian religious groups constructed looser hierarchies than the orthodox Church. Some, such as the Society of Friends, did away with a formal structure altogether. Most permitted married clergy, pastors or elders. It was no longer necessary to have a priest as an intermediary between a person and God.

As people were empowered to read and interpret the Bible for themselves, there was a consequent decline in clerical authority.

These centuries saw many social and political changes, not least due to the Industrial Revolution and the development of science. In Europe, the French Revolution with its ideas of liberty, equality and fraternity had contributed to change in the course of European thought. Massive social changes and reforms were under way. Men and women (eventually) were enfranchised. In the twentieth century, two world wars led to the collapse of the old social orders. State provision or support for housing, education and health care were factors in the improvement of people's lives in many European countries. Education and the promulgation of scientific discoveries led to a more informed populace who were prepared to make decisions for themselves. By the 1950s Pope John XXIII said that it was time to open the windows of the Catholic Church and let in some fresh air.

CHAPTER TEN:

THE TWENTIETH CENTURY: THE PROTECTION OF SEMEN CONTINUES

The next stage on the trail of semen is that of the Second Vatican Council (Vatican II), called by Pope John XXIII in 1959. The council was hailed as a new epiphany for the orthodox Catholic Church. However, there was no epiphany for women, or for semen. The status of semen remained inviolate. The retention of semen by the celibate male continued and the authority of the male celibate to define and explain 'truth' remained. There were no changes to institutional celibacy or to women's position. Despite some fine words during the Second Vatican Council, there remained little support for women's equality in the celibate tradition.

Pope John XXIII (1958–63) and Pope Paul VI (1963–78) endorsed the theory of women's equality, but women were only permitted to participate in the life of the Church as long as they did not hold power. When women raise gender issues they challenge the sexual theology of Christianity, the fantasies surrounding semen, stereotypical images of woman and of man, the idea of male celibates' access to 'truth' and ultimately the traditional power structure itself. Women are equal and necessary as long as they keep their place. Women's subordination runs not only through the history and culture of the Church, but 'in the conscious fibre of many men and women who justify this bias as natural that is, sanctioned by grace'.[1]

Levels of participation of the laity did increase following the Second Vatican Council. The clear division in the 'Fortress

Church' between the sacred and the profane became blurred as a result of new notions of ministry arising from Vatican II. Priests and people had to adjust to new symbols and notions of sacredness. Women accessed sacred spaces for the first time. However, notions of impurity associated with women's natural functions could not be swept aside overnight. For example, some Catholic women continued to be 'churched' (cleansed) after giving birth well into the 1970s. Distinctions between clergy and laity were to remain. The Pope stressed that the pastoral tasks of lay people may not obscure the priestly ministry, that there must be a delimitation of responsibilities and a distinction between tasks.

There was no structural change to support new models of priesthood. It follows therefore that no fundamental shift of power occurred. Power remained with the celibate hierarchy. Yet the authority of the Pope, and priests, declined in line with the loss of papal authority following the encyclical *Humanae Vitae* (July 1968), which provides the most significant staging post for our trail of semen in the twentieth century. We shall look at this in detail in a later chapter. Suffice to say here that the majority of English Catholics were at variance with official Church teachings on sexual matters, especially with regard to contraception, divorce and abortion.[2] Many Catholics, in good conscience, decided to make their own decisions about their sexual lives. The overall effect of official Church teachings on sexual matters was that matters of personal sexuality were removed from the exclusive domain of Church Fathers and the clergy. Catholics became much more aware of the 'supremacy of individual conscience'; Confession went into decline, and with it one of the most powerful tools with which to control the laity disappeared. Once their authoritarian roles were gone, many priests were disempowered.

Sharp (1993) interviewed a sample of English Catholic priests and identified conflict in the priestly role as a factor in stress and, ultimately, exodus from the priesthood. Priests dealing with the everyday experiences and beliefs of ordinary Catholics found that they were ministering to their congregation with only one eye on Rome and its orthodox doctrines regarding sexual matters. The majority of the priests interviewed found themselves in conflict with the sexual theology of the Vatican and the reality of the daily lives of their parishioners. Few condemned contraception, abortion, divorce and remarriage, as required by official doctrine. Most said that there were 'exceptions' and/or 'circumstances' which allowed for contraception, abortion, divorce and remarriage. The majority also said that they had no objection to married priests. Exposed to the same questions of authority as the laity, some found themselves caught 'between a rock and a hard place' – between the 'official line' and a laity which largely refuted the authority of Rome.[3]

A significant finding was that none of the priests could offer a definitive, operational, explanation of celibacy. Several priests made a distinction between the law of celibacy and the ideal of chastity. For some it meant non-marriage and periodic abstinence. Several priests felt that chastity was a 'gift' not given to all, and a vocation to the priesthood did not necessarily mean a vocation to celibacy. The scene was set for personal conflict or compromise; to stay or to go.

Following the Second Vatican Council, the last half of the twentieth century saw more than 100,000 Catholic priests leave the ministry.[4] That was almost a quarter of all the active priests in the world. It is estimated that forty-two per cent of all American priests leave within twenty-five years of ordination. This translates into the exodus of half of all American priests under sixty years of age. Spain lost 7,000 priests, from 28,000. In France, priest numbers dropped to 25,000 by the year 2000, from 40,000 in 1969.[5] Michael Gaine, professor of sociology at Christ's and Notre Dame College Liverpool, examined statistics for Britain, gleaned from the *Catholic Directory* over the years from 1968 to the end of the twentieth century, and found a steady decline in numbers.

That mandatory celibacy might have something to do with the exodus of priests[6] is revealed in the Vatican's own *Annuarium Statisticum Ecclesiae* (1986). For example, there were 46,302 dispensations for priests to marry between 1963 and 1983, and it is supposed that for every priest who gets a dispensation there is another who was refused or never bothered to try.[7] In the twenty-first century the decline continues. Between the middle of the twentieth century and the second decade of the twenty-first century the number of priests worldwide declined from 419,728 to 414,313.[8]

As in previous centuries, violations against celibacy continued; and it is clear that many priests do not maintain a celibate existence. From the 1970s to the end of the twentieth century, there were heterosexual and homosexual transgressions against celibacy; and paedophilia and other sexual compromises. In *Shattered Vows* (1991), David Rice uncovered a catalogue of violations against celibacy, which caused great pain for the priests, women and children involved. By the 1990s it was estimated that up to fifty per cent of American priests had violated their celibate state. A further consideration is that by the end of the century, due to the alarming number of incidents of abuse by priests, the celibate man had become an object of suspicion. During the twentieth century, attitudes towards sexuality became more broad-minded, and the Catholic ideal of asexual or anti-sexual asceticism appeared more symptomatic of cultural or personal psychosis than of spirituality. Catholic prohibitions surrounding sexual activity seemed unhealthy and restraining.

Nevertheless, the hierarchy continued to enforce celibacy in spite of the damage it appeared to cause many priests, and despite the role it may have played in mounting examples of sexual abuse.

Following revelations during the United States Conference of Bishops as early as 1993 about violations of celibacy, American bishops again asked the Pope to discuss the question of celibacy. Legal proceedings taken against Catholic priests in the United States and England focused attention on the sexual abuse of children by priests. Concerns about mandatory celibacy also raise issues of human rights, the lagging number of vocations, clerical alienation from the people served and negativity towards sexuality in general. The response from the celibate hierarchy has been one of denial. John Paul II, in his 'Message for Vocations', Sunday 2 May 1993, refuted suggestions that obligatory celibacy is the cause of any such problems. The Pope considered that the 'crisis' of vocations is not about mandatory celibacy, but due to the

> ambiguities of progress, the pseudo-values, the snares and deceptions which certain civilizations make shine before our eyes, the temptations of materialism and passing ideologies.[9]

The Pope said that the cause of the 'crisis' in the priesthood and with vocations is a questioning, a turning away from traditional orthodoxy. Obstacles to celibacy and to vocations will be overcome by fostering the 'right conditions'. These conditions include a return to a strict sexual morality, and an acceptance of the orthodox 'truths'. Mandatory celibacy has thus become not merely an imposed discipline, but a symbol of holy orders and of orthodoxy. Nevertheless, Pope John Paul II created a special provision for some Protestant ministers who chose to become Catholic but wanted to remain active in ministry. They were kept out of the limelight.[10]

In *The Tablet*, 14 March 1992, it was reported that Bishop Davidek of Prague ordained eighty married men to the priesthood by 1992 when Czechoslovakia was under communist rule.[11] The total number of married priests in the former Soviet Union is unknown. At the end of the twentieth century it was evident that married priests existed in the Catholic Church, but numbers remained unclear. The Movement for the Ordination of married Men suggest that the Vatican agenda is directed towards ensuring that there should not be an active married priesthood within the Latin rite of the Church, except by way of exception, and that with a low profile.[12] Consequently, most of these men remain in chaplaincies with little involvement in parish life. In 1992, the decision of the General Synod of the Church of England to approve the ordination of women priests prompted the exodus of a number of married priests from the

Anglican Church. Some sought refuge in the Catholic Church. Pope Benedict XVI (2005–13) took the involvement of married priests a step further. He created a new 'virtual' diocese independent of geography. In this new diocese Protestant priests and their faith communities were able to become Catholic, yet the married priests were retained.

In the light of the growing clamour for changes to institutional celibacy, and the calls for married priests and women priests, there is a significant shift of emphasis away from celibacy as a discipline, to that of 'sign and symbol'. The orthodox position is that

> Celibacy is a freely chosen dynamic state, usually vowed, that involves an honest and sustained attempt to live without direct sexual gratification in order to serve others productively or for a spiritual motive.[13]

As early as the 1960s, in the encyclical *Sacerdotalis Caelibatus*,[14] Paul VI talks of celibacy as 'a brilliant jewel and retains its value undiminished even in our time, when mentality and structures have undergone profound change'. He talks of the 'golden law of sacred celibacy'[15] and counters all objections by offering Christ as the model and the ideal. He links celibacy with sanctity, describing it as 'a badge to charity', an example 'by which man expresses his own unique greatness'.[16]

However, John Paul II admitted in July 1993 that celibacy was not a law promulgated by Christ, that the essential nature of the priesthood did not require celibacy, and that the early Church did allow married priests.[17] However, he went on to say that celibacy was the most coherent way of life for holy orders.

Denying that the celibate was holier than other men, he nevertheless continued with the notion that the male virgin is almost angelic. Given that a soul in Paradise would live in an asexual existence, celibacy was the 'most similar' way of life on earth and therefore the most 'exemplary'. Such notions depend heavily on the truth of Genesis, the doctrine of original sin, and the association between sex and sin. These in turn depend upon the biologically determined theology for their continued legitimacy. The Pope's discourse provides a continuity with the notion that the male virgin is almost angelic and therefore most able to define and explain truth.

The Pope also stressed that 'the needs of priesthood' are better served by celibacy; that celibacy became a rule in the Western Church as the 'maturing of the ecclesial conscience' made it aware that celibacy best served the priesthood. No mention was made of the ongoing resistance to enforced celibacy. The reality is that institutional celibacy serves the interests of an elite hierarchy, not the interests of many priests. Therefore 'the needs of the priesthood' may be seen as synonymous with the needs of the Church hierarchy. Emphasis on celibacy as a sign or symbol contains the public debate, as does the insistence that only a man can 'image Christ'. The insistence of celibacy as a symbol of holy orders prevents any debate about optional celibacy and effectively prevents any real debate about married priests or women priests.

Certainly, it cannot be denied that celibacy freely chosen can be considered as a sign or symbol. That some men and women achieve celibacy thus defined is a sign of self-denial and dedication to others in a sexually explicit world. Nevertheless, in stressing celibacy as a sign or symbol, the Church focuses on the positive intentions of the individual while omitting any debate about celibacy as a discipline. Further, as the institution of celibacy is also an integral part of hierarchical power in the Church, to talk of celibacy merely as a sign or symbol is to leave the underlying issue of power untouched. Interestingly, the celibate female is not elevated to the realms of the angelic with its privileged access to 'truth'.

To date there has been no public discussion about the achievements or compromises of celibacy. In the absence of open discussion, some priests use the secrecy of the confessional to share their celibate successes and failures. Others continue to struggle on alone, some becoming embittered in the process. The taboo surrounding sexuality and celibacy remains.[18] Yet, on the positive side, there may be much to be learned about sexuality. Any sexual/celibate adjustment is usually a private matter. A priest's sexual/celibate life may only become visible through a scandal which comes to public attention. Further, that individual priests have not come to terms with their own sexuality raises the question of how celibates can therefore claim to be the 'experts on humanity' or on issues of sexual morality, as proposed by Pope John Paul II in 1993 in the encyclical *Veritatis Splendor*.[19] What is questionable is whether the celibate can claim any knowledge of sexual love, or have any understanding of the role of sexual activity in long-term relationships.

Both the official Church and individual priests perpetuate the taboo surrounding sexuality and celibacy. Statements on celibacy are typically defensive and based on the assumption that priests are consistent to their vows.[20] The Catholic priesthood probably holds within its experience specific information about abstinence and self-control. But to ask a priest about his sexual/celibate adjustment is to invite secrecy, denial and mystery.[21] This is probably because many priests do not understand sexuality in the broad definition of the word – a mode of coming to terms with one's sexual energies.

A further issue which may prevent informed debate is the apparent lack of awareness among the clergy of the ideological and theological underpinnings of celibacy.[22] There is scant evidence to suppose that many celibates link the institution of celibacy to power or the oppression of women in the Church. There is, however, one paper worthy of note presented by James Francis Stafford, Archbishop of Denver, at the Symposium *'Pastores Dabo Vobis'* (On The Priestly Life), in Rome in 1992.

Stafford crystallised the negativity towards and contamination by sex, the inferior position of women, the superiority of virginity, and the external rather than internal elements of spirituality.[23] The reported shock and horror with which Stafford's paper was received by many of the 'expert' delegates highlights their lack of awareness of the origins of sexual theology, the Church's discourse on women or biblical and historical scholarship. These issues would have to be raised if celibacy were to be debated. The lack of awareness of such key issues prevents informed debate.

Institutional celibacy was the final moulding of the sacerdotal caste system. It remains not only as a significant staging post in the trail of semen down through the ages, but as a bulwark for the fantasies surrounding semen. As celibacy came to mean perpetual sexual abstinence rather than merely non-marriage, celibacy and continence came to mean the same thing. It was a sexual shift which transferred power and authority into the hands of the celibates. An elite group of celibate males held all power and authority in the Church and imposed their will on the majority of priests. From its inception, institutional celibacy was strongly resisted by many priests, and violations against celibacy have been a constant feature of institutional celibacy. Much damage has been done to many priests because of mandatory celibacy. It is an apparatus of power that functions as a system of control imposed by an elite group on the majority of the clergy. It is a relation of power in which some men, subordinate to other men, are forced to do what they otherwise would not have chosen to do.

In the twenty-first century, institutional celibacy remains the backbone of the patriarchal Church. A patriarchal theology supported by patriarchal structures operates in the interest of an elite group of powerful men as it enables them to control priests, other men and women. The presumed access to 'truth' by the celibate hierarchy continues. It follows therefore that the static and unchanging nature of Catholic 'truth' must be maintained, and resistance in this group to a revised sexual theology will be strong. Optional celibacy will be resisted as will equality for women, for both undermine the 'truth' of orthodox sexual theology. Institutional celibacy, patriarchy and sexual theology are mutually supporting and sustaining. Institutional celibacy is therefore a vehicle of oppression in the Church.

Contemporary strategies employed by the elite group to contain dissent are similar to those used to contain the debate on contraception. Control of public discourse is maintained as debate is denied. The discourse has been moved away from that of 'discipline' to that of 'sign and symbol' using the politics of piety with no reference to the underlying issue of power. The strength of the public discourse, and the refusal to debate the issue, indicates the existence of alternative discourses, points of resistance within the Church. A call to priesthood is not necessarily a call to celibacy, even though it is currently presented as a 'state freely chosen . . . a sign and symbol'. In the absence of a public discourse and the changing explanations of celibacy, it is unsurprising that individual priests have differing understandings of celibacy. In the author's research, it was evident that priests found it difficult to come up with a clear definition or explanation of celibacy.

CHAPTER ELEVEN:

THE RETURN TO TRADITIONAL ORTHODOXY

As we saw earlier, the Second Vatican Council and the papal encyclical *Humanae Vitae*[1] were two of the most the most significant staging posts in tracing the trail of semen through the twentieth century. Many Catholic women awaited the publication of *Humanae Vitae* in the hope that the contraceptive pill would be permitted. In his attempt to protect both semen and papal authority, the Pope (Paul VI) seriously undermined both the Church's control of women's sexuality and its own authority in the sexual lives of married people. *Humanae Vitae* forced Catholics to make distinctions between 'infallible' and 'non-infallible' pronouncements by the Pope. The days of a largely unreflective acceptance of papal infallibility by the Catholic laity, together with 'blind obedience' to Rome, were at an end. Catholic women, and men, were driven to ask themselves crucial questions about their allegiance to the Church and the authority of the Pope in such matters. Catholics did not confess to using artificial methods of birth control or declined to participate in confession at all, using 'supremacy of conscience' as their ultimate guide. In matters of sexual morality, the Catholic laity began to temper the sexual theology of the Church with the reality of their own lived experience.

The development of the first oral contraceptives sent shock waves through the Vatican. Traditional arguments against contraception were underpinned by the concern to protect semen, the 'divine liquid'. Despite biological proof that semen did not contain the whole foetus in embryo, but merely contained the fertiliser, arguments against contraception continued to focus on 'spilling the seed' other than in the 'correct vessel', the womb. With the contraceptive pill, there was no hindrance to the deposit of semen in the 'correct vessel'. Dissenters in the Church asked for a rethink on the Church's position on contraceptives. In 1963 Pope John XXIII established a commission of six European non-theologians to study questions of birth control and population. Pope Paul VI, following John Paul XXIII's death, expanded the commission. Members of the commission included theologians, legal experts, historians, sociologists, doctors, obstetricians and married couples.

Despite a majority in favour of recommending birth control to the Pope, four dissenting theologians enabled the recommendation to 'fail'.[2] Pope Paul VI became convinced that to allow artificial birth control would be to undermine the authority of past popes and would question the Church's sexual theology. For the traditionalists, papal authority was a key issue. Did the papal encyclical *Casti Connubii*,[3] which denounced birth control in the 1930s, retain its authority as it stood; or could a modified version of its teaching be acceptable as a 'legitimate development'. The Pope finally decided to ban artificial birth control, against the recommendations of the commission. The opportunity for a radical rethink of traditional sexual theology had been missed, with damaging consequences for the Church.

A significant factor in patriarchy is who controls reproduction? Who is to control women and their bodies? With the introduction of the contraceptive pill, women were no longer at the mercy of unreliable methods of contraception and had (potentially) the means to control their own fertility. The power to decide on reproduction had shifted to women themselves. The 'rhythm method' or what the Catholic Church calls 'natural family planning' had been permissible since the 1930s. At first glance, the difference between the (later) ban on the contraceptive pill and the admissibility of the rhythm method lay in the hair-splitting division between means and ends; but there is a significant difference between the two. With the rhythm method, the use of condoms or coitus interruptus, the ultimate power to use contraception and the choice of method is with the man. Hence, the power over reproduction remains largely with the man. If the man chooses not to cooperate, he can insist on his conjugal 'rights' and even use force in the process. With the contraceptive pill, for the first time in history, the power over reproduction is with the woman.

Church Fathers searched in vain for new explanations for their centuries-old ban on contraception. Concern for the safe delivery of semen into the correct vessel continued. This should no longer have been an issue, for with the contraceptive pill semen had free access to the womb. Condoms, withdrawal (coitus interruptus), and other forms of contraception had been forbidden as they prevented semen from reaching the correct vessel – the womb. Attention turned to the 'rhythm method' or what the Church prefers to call 'natural family planning'. The explanation for the ban on contraception now became that of 'naturalness'. The rhythm method involves periods of abstinence; intercourse takes place in the woman's infertile periods and at no other time. This is said to take note of nature's natural rhythms and is a legitimate use of a contraceptive method. All other forms of contraception are 'unnatural', therefore illicit. For most women, the reasons for the use of contraception in whatever form were more important than the mere mechanics used to achieve the same end.[4] The attempt to retain control of women's reproduction failed as many Catholic women rejected the ban. This significant change of emphasis from a male-dominated role in reproduction more clearly revealed the attempt to continue the control of women and their bodies in a patriarchal Church. The ban on contraception had more to do with the control of women, and the protection of semen than it ever had to do with children.

The undeniable fact was that men and women were naturally called to equal partnership in procreation. However, a natural partnership threatened a patriarchal theology rooted in biological determinism, and an appeal to the 'natural law' that should have led to an examination of a sexual theology in which the superiority of man was dependent on erroneous ideas about semen. Women could no longer be denied their equal part in reproduction, no longer be considered a mere vessel for men's seed. Such an examination should have led to a reconstruction of woman as equal with man. The discovery of the ovum in 1827 by Professor Karl Ernst von Baer should have led to a radical rethink of the Church's sexual theology, with its roots in the fantasies surrounding semen. No longer the only factor in reproduction, semen lost its status overnight, going from what Aquinas called 'that divine liquid', which contained the whole foetus in embryo, to that of fertiliser.[5]

The Second Vatican Council used a more conciliatory tone towards women. However, any encouragement engendered by the Council document *Gaudium et Spes* (1965)[6], and others favourable to women, was tempered by the decision to ban artificial birth control. *Gaudium et Spes* 'allowed' intercourse for the 'mutual well-being' of the married couple. That a couple may 'bond' through sexual intercourse was a new departure from traditional teaching. For centuries, the laity had been told to avoid pleasure when engaging in sexual intercourse and to only indulge in sexual intercourse in order to procreate. *Gaudium et Spes* also talked of 'responsible parenthood', a euphemism for family planning. 'Responsible family planning' was condoned, but only through the use of 'approved methods' of contraception – the rhythm method and/or abstinence. The passage of semen into the correct vessel must continue unimpeded.

The debate on contraception had taken place within the confines of the commission. The recommendations of the majority report were ignored, hijacked by the Roman conservative old guard. An apparently reluctant and indecisive pontiff was encouraged to maintain the status quo. But, nothing would be the same again. With regard to contraception as with other areas of sexual morality, what was becoming clear to the Catholic population was the lack of knowledge, expertise, understanding or willingness to listen by the Church celibates. Contraception and other issues of sexual morality became questions for the individual conscience. Catholics began to question issues fundamental to power and authority – celibacy, sexual theology, and the nature, role and status of women in the Church. Far from strengthening papal authority, and with it patriarchal power in the Church, the decision to ban the contraceptive pill achieved exactly the opposite effect. The issue of contraception highlights male control of women and their bodies. With the development of the contraceptive pill, women, no longer at the mercy of unreliable methods of contraception, had the means to control their own fertility. In effect, the power to decide on reproduction had shifted to women themselves. This power shift underpins the whole debate about contraception. It raises questions of who is to control reproduction. Or, put another way, who is to control women and their bodies? Women or men?

With the arrival of Karol Wojtyla as Pope John Paul II, in 1979, the stage was set for a retrenchment to pre-Vatican II days. With the Vatican's chief theologian, Cardinal Joseph Ratzinger, the future Benedict XVI, John Paul II set about unmaking much of the modernisation project since the council. He issued emphatic rulings condemning abortion, birth control and homosexuality. He dismissed calls for the relaxation of the celibacy rules for priests, and for the ordination of women. He criticised liberation theology and surrounded himself with dyed-in-the-wool conservatives like Ratzinger. For the clergy, questioning traditional teachings, even gently, became a potential career-ender.

John Paul II emphasised stereotypical, patriarchal images of women. This is evident in the Pope's response to calls for women to access the priesthood. In June 1994, the Pope spoke out 'definitively' about the ordination of women. In *De Sacerdotali Ordinatione Vitis Tantum Reservanda* (On Reserving Priestly Ministry to Men Alone), he states that the Church 'has no authority whatsoever' to ordain women. In the Catholic Church priestly ordination '*has from the beginning been reserved to men alone*'.[7]

In the absence of theological explanations to exclude women, the Pope offers certain 'fundamental reasons' to exclude women: Christ chose only men as apostles, the constant practice of the Church and the 'living teaching authority which has consistently held that the exclusion of women from priesthood is in accordance with God's plan for his Church'. Finally, 'A woman cannot image Christ.'[8]

The exclusion of women from the priesthood is merely because she is not a man. The 'living teaching authority' is in accordance with patriarchy and relies on the possession of semen as 'proof' for man's superiority. To suggest that this is 'God's plan' is presumptuous.

In declaring his judgement is 'to be definitively held', the Pope goes as close to declaring his judgement as infallible as he is able. The pontiff used a language of centralising control and imposed authority by effectively insinuating the exercise of infallibility without actually invoking it.[9] The exclusion of women from priesthood is considered a matter of faith, not of discipline. In the case of married men it is a question of discipline, whereas in the case of women it is a matter of faith, a divine ordinance of the Pope.[10] Pope John Paul II forbade any further discussion on the matter.

Following Vatican II, in the period known as the post-conciliar years, it was evident that dissent was no longer containable. Traditionalists thought that the Church was in a 'crisis'. They said that 'irresponsible theologians' confused the ordinary, simple faithful with 'their anti-Roman speculations'. Moral theologians were, they explained, guilty of confusing Catholics on birth control, abortion and homosexuality. With the administration of John Paul II, they found a champion for their cause. Dissent, an ongoing feature of the Church, usually centred on power, authority and the papacy,[11] and traditional strategies for containment were employed. The power of the papacy was strengthened as collegiality was subverted; a new form of confession of faith now required total assent to the non-infallible utterances of the Pope. A particular oath of fidelity to the Supreme Pontiff was required.[12] The nomination of bishops and office holders was centralised. Eminent theologians who questioned the totality of orthodox 'truths' were disciplined. For example, Edward Schillebeeckx who questioned the literal truth of the Resurrection and the Virgin Birth, was publicly accused of heresy. He also questioned the Church's position on celibacy, women's ordination, and the fixed and immutable doctrines of orthodoxy. In 1974, the theologian Küng had also questioned the doctrine of infallibility, and criticised the Pope's rigidity in morals and dogma. In 1979, Küng was pronounced unfit to teach Roman Catholic doctrine. It became apparent that the first question asked of any theologian was not their ability to enlighten, but whether they conformed to traditional orthodoxy.

With the pontificate of John Paul II, overt absolutism had returned to the Church. The attempt at Vatican II to promote collegiality and co-responsibility in the College of Cardinals had been revised, and reduced to 'purely practical arrangements' of no collegial or theological significance.[13] In the 1993 encyclical *Veritatis Splendor*,[14] the Pope demands obedience, total assent and submission to all papal utterances. John Paul II's answer to loss of authority and control was to return to a monarchical concept of the Church; to confirm male superiority and women's subordinate position. In *Veritatis Splendor* the nature and place of women is clearly laid out. The Pope reaffirms traditional depictions of women's 'natural' or 'divinely mandated' roles of mother, virgin and martyr. The Pope's appeal to the natural law reveals a desire to maintain existing arrangements in the Church, which favour men, and from which women are 'naturally' excluded. The emphasis on the natural law of Aquinas exposes a patriarchal mindset trapped in a pre-Renaissance morality.

In 1979, the Pontifical Council for the Family was charged by the Holy Father with producing this confessor's aid.

> The Church has always taught the intrinsic evil of contraception, that is, of every marital act intentionally rendered unfruitful. This teaching is to be held as definitive and irreformable. Contraception is gravely opposed to marital chastity; it is contrary to the good of the transmission of life (the procreative

aspect of matrimony), and to the reciprocal self-giving of the spouses (the unitive aspect of matrimony); it harms true love and denies the sovereign role of God in the transmission of human life.[15]

More difficult to hear was any condemnation of the continued oppression of and violence against women in many parts of the world and the abandonment of millions of babies, especially girls, in certain countries where girls are valued less than boys.

The imperative to continue the control of women, their bodies and reproduction was a notable feature of John Paul II's administration. The Pope spoke about contraception at every opportunity. In 1983, Pope John Paul II said,

> Contraception is to be judged objectively so profoundly unlawful as never to be, for any reason, justified. To think or to say the contrary is equal to maintaining that, in human life, situations may arise in which it is lawful not to recognize God as God.[15]

Despite the increased volume of pronouncements concerning contraception, many women continued to decide about contraception for themselves. In the face of a losing battle against the contraceptive pill the Pope turned his attention to the rhythm method. Augustine, one of the greatest Fathers of the Church, abhorred this method of contraception. He was convinced that it turned men into 'pimps', 'whoremongers' and 'adulterers'.[16] The Pope on the other hand tried to persuade women that it is a recipe for marital harmony. In his encyclical *Familiaris Consortio*,[17] he asserted that salvation and marital happiness are essentially based on practising the right method of contraception. Peace and harmony will be maintained in the family if family size is controlled by the rhythm method rather than any other.

At the end of the twentieth century, there was no change in the sexual theology of the Catholic Christian Church. The concern continues to be the protection of semen and male control over conception. The Pope's concern was not about marital harmony; it was a concern to protect semen. The ejaculation of semen in any place other than the womb is the main concern in the ban on masturbation, coitus interruptus and all forms of contraception. The sexual act must be controlled in order to ensure the delivery of semen into the correct vessel (the womb), in the proper manner and for the right reasons. In the light of current knowledge about the ovum and of sperm (merely as a fertiliser), sexual theology, rooted as it is in the fantasies surrounding semen, is seriously undermined. To continue with this discredited theology is to sacrifice 'truth' to the ideology of patriarchy.

It appears that John Paul II realised the importance of maintaining patriarchal attitudes and societies worldwide. Not content to confine his discourse to the Catholic Church, he attempted to control the international discourse about women. On the eve of the Fourth International Conference on Women in Beijing (1995) Mrs Gertrude Mogella, the General Secretary of the conference, was given a written message from the Pope, which stated some of the basic points of Church teaching with regard to women's issues. Themes from the document provided the basis for the Pope's Letter to Women (1995).[18] In this letter it is made clear that women are an anomaly, a 'mystery', different from men, who are the norm. That the letter was written at all suggests that the centuries-long indifference to women can no longer be maintained. Persistent pressure from the women's movement in general, and from the Catholic women's movement within the Church, has forced acknowledgement of women's contribution to society and to the Church. Women are knocking on the doors of the Vatican demanding to be heard.

The dilemma facing the Pope is as it has always been: how to accommodate women and at the same time exclude them. In his Letter to Women, the Pope reminds women of their position as 'helper' to men. 'Woman's special "genius" is service to others . . . Service is in no way prejudicial to women,' assures the Pope. 'A certain diversity of roles . . . is an expression of what is specific to being male and female.' Women are reminded that Mary is the highest expression of the 'feminine genius'. She called herself the 'handmaid of the Lord' (Luke 1:38) '. . . for her, "to reign" is "to serve"! Her service is "to reign" '.[19]

In line with traditional stereotypes, the Pope supported his continued exclusion of women by a reductionist theory of 'complementarity'. Woman is 'complementary' to man. She is everything man is not.

> Womanhood and manhood are complementary not only from the physical and psychological points of view but also from the ontological.[19]

However, biological, psychological and ontological explanations for differences between the sexes have been discredited. Social differences based on biological differences are in effect inequalities justified by a belief in the superiority of the male of the species. The Pope's attempt to reconcile the rhetoric of exclusion to social processes of accommodation reveals yet again a patriarchal mindset, which presumes to explain and define women through their relations with men. It is another brick in the wall of the Vatican fortifications designed to repel women and protect the status quo. The hopeful era, for many Catholics, following the Vatican Council soon evaporated as it became clear that successive popes would reinforce orthodoxy. Efforts were made to modernise some traditional practices and the actual teachings of Jesus continued to be interpreted in more liberal and egalitarian ways in many parishes. However, liberation theologians, especially those in South America, were not alone in being discouraged by the Vatican.

After John Paul II died in 2005, Cardinal Ratzinger took over as Pope Benedict, and the conservative counteroffensive continued. Indeed, it intensified. Benedict made clear that he saw his primary mission not as extending and enlarging the Catholic Church, but as purifying it. He did not mean dealing with the child-abuse scandal in which he was implicated by his failure to take appropriate steps to deal with the matter. He meant casting off extraneous growths – presumably the outcomes of Vatican II – and getting the Church back to what he saw as its proper roots. If this process alienated some current and former members of the faith, so be it. Benedict said numerous times that the Church might well be healthier if it was smaller.

The Vatican eased restrictions on the Latin Mass and invited back into the Church some excommunicated members of the Society of Pius X, an ultra-conservative group dedicated to reversing the Second Vatican Council. The Pope criticised the 'culture of relativism' in modern societies, and 'the anarchic freedom that wrongly passes for true freedom'. Under the German Pope Benedict, a small, primarily Italian clique of yes-men – people with no sympathy for the calls to reform – were allowed to come into power. In an interview in 2011 with the German news magazine *Der Spiegel*, Hans Küng, the dissident Swiss theologian who knew Pope Benedict when they were both young priests in Germany, made a telling comparison between him and Vladimir Putin, pointing out that the two leaders had inherited a series of democratic reforms they set out to reverse. Putin and Benedict both 'placed their former associates in key positions and sidelined those they didn't like'. Küng said that one could draw other parallels: the disempowerment of the Russian Parliament and the Vatican Synod of Bishops, the degradation of Russian provincial governors and of Catholic bishops to make them nothing but recipients of orders, a conformist 'nomenclature' and a resistance to real reforms. They are partly responsible for the stagnation that stifles every attempt at modernisation of the Church system.[20]

The strategy of circling the wagons was evident in the Vatican's response to the child-abuse scandal. The office of the Congregation for the Doctrine of the Faith, led by Cardinal Ratzinger, had authority over sexual-abuse cases. Ratzinger was responsible for dealing with the matter, but did nothing despite having extensive evidence that sexual abuse had occurred. For the two decades he was in charge of the congregation, the Cardinal failed to act even as the cases of abuse mounted in the United States, Australia, Ireland and elsewhere. It was not until July 2008 that Ratzinger, as Pope Benedict, finally apologised for the acts of paedophiles in the Church.

In the *New Yorker* of 12 February 2013, David Clohessy, executive director of the 12,000-strong survivors' network of those abused by priests, said,

> He knows more about clergy sex crimes and cover-ups than anyone else in the Church, yet he has done precious little to protect children.

In *The Guardian* of 13 February 2013, John Kelly, one of the founders of Ireland's Survivors of Child Abuse group, said when Benedict stepped down as pontiff,

> I'm afraid to say Pope Benedict won't be missed, as the Vatican continued to block proper investigations into the abuse scandals during his term in office. . . . For us, he broke his word.[21]

At the beginning of the twenty-first century, Pope Benedict continued with the concern to protect semen, and ensure delivery into the correct vessel, at any cost. While on his way to Africa in 2009, the Pope said that the Aids problem on the continent (in sub-Saharan Africa alone 22 million people are suffering from HIV infection and Aids) could not be resolved by distributing condoms. The use of condoms will not stop the spread of the disease, but may make the situation even worse. . . . The way to stop the disease, he said, was through sexual monogamy.

The Pope stated that

> The most effective presence on the front in the battle against HIV/Aids is the Catholic Church and her institutions.[22]

There was a strong response to the Pope's statements. The French Foreign Ministry was sharply critical, saying, 'Such remarks put in danger public health policy and imperative needs regarding the protection of human life.'

Belgian Health Minister Laurette Onkelinx said, 'Ratzinger's comments . . . reflect a dangerous doctrinaire vision; the Pope is making matters worse.'

John O'Brien, of Catholics for Choice, said, 'It took the Church hierarchy 359 years to stop continuing the line taken by their predecessors on Galileo. We hope that this error does not take so long to change.'[23]

Ratzinger stood down as Pope in February 2013. The new Pope Francis appears to have a less doctrinaire approach. Nevertheless, when in the Philippines, Francis restated the Catholic Church's traditional position on contraception, but tempered this by stating that using a condom to preserve life, reduce the risk of infection and avoid death could be a responsible act – even outside marriage.

> In certain cases, where the intention is to reduce the risk of infection, it can nevertheless be a first step on the way to another, more humane sexuality.[24]

Could this be the light at the end of the tunnel?

The Second Vatican Council was an attempt to bring the Catholic Church up to date. While women were 'allowed' to enter sacred spaces for the first time, and even to distribute Communion, there was no change in the patriarchal attitudes and organisation of the Church. The encyclical *Humanae Vitae*, which prohibited the use of the contraceptive pill, led to unintended consequences for the Church hierarchy and the ordinary clergy. Clerical power over the sexual lives of many Catholics was compromised as Catholics asked themselves questions about the authority of the Pope in such matters. Concern for the delivery of semen into the 'correct vessel' in the 'correct manner' dominated discussions about use of the contraceptive pill. The dilemma was that with the contraceptive pill semen continued to have unimpeded access to the 'vessel'. So, what was the problem? Pope Paul felt that earlier papal decisions on the matter – that is, papal authority – would be called into question if he accepted the recommendations of the panel and allowed use of the contraceptive pill. His decision to ban the contraceptive pill did exactly the opposite of what was intended. Advances in biology which had shown that the 'seed' is in the woman, and that semen is only the carrier for the fertiliser, made no change to the status of semen. The underlying concern was who was to control conception – woman or man?

Dissent in the Church continued through the following decades, but with the pontificate of John Paul II absolutism returned to the Church. He and his successor dismantled much of what had been achieved by the Second Vatican Council. At the beginning of the twenty-first century, Pope Benedict continued with the underlying concern to protect the free passage of semen into the 'correct vessel'. Evidence for this is his pronouncements on the use of condoms to prevent the spread of HIV.

At this point it will be useful to reflect on our journey, before we consider the negative impact of patriarchy and patriarchal ideas that continue to have an impact on many women's lives in the twenty-first century.

CHAPTER TWELVE:

PATRIARCHY DISGUISED AS 'TRADITION' OR 'CULTURE'

We have followed the trail of semen through the orthodox Christian Church, but there is little doubt that a similar journey could be made through the other patriarchal world religions. This could be the subject of further research. What we have uncovered here is that the justification for patriarchy in the public and private spheres ultimately depends on the fantasies surrounding semen. Once these fantasies have been exposed, patriarchal beliefs about male superiority collapse like a house of cards. What is remarkable is that the discovery of the ovum has made little difference to patriarchal attitudes and structures. There has been no reassessment of age-old myths, resulting stereotypes, roles and responsibilities by any of the main patriarchal religions. In many religions, cultures and institutions, the ideology of patriarchy is so entrenched and institutionalised that it will take a long time for notions of male dominance to change.

The primary justification for male superiority was lost in the mists of time. It is doubtful that many men or women know about the fantasies surrounding semen, or know how these fantasies underpin presumptions about male superiority. Nevertheless, patriarchal systems, institutions and religions have elevated men and controlled women based on these assumptions. In the twenty-first century, women worldwide continue to be subjected to violence, forced marriage, early death, honour killings, genital mutilation and rape. Many patriarchal societies and religions continue to refuse women access to family planning, contraception, safe abortions or divorce. The increasing independence of women in the Western world is not the experience of millions of women in other parts of the world. Patriarchal beliefs and organisations continue to exist, justified by the fantastic beliefs surrounding semen, with consequent stereotypes, roles and responsibilities. The evidence is that women continue to be the largest group of underdogs the world has ever seen.

Some women have experienced a level of mitigation in the worst effects of patriarchy, particularly in the Western world, but there is an over-abundance of evidence to illustrate the continued subordination of women worldwide. Beatrix Campbell[1] suggests that the belief that women and men are on an evolving cultural journey towards equality (even in the West) is misguided. The evidence is that progress towards equality in many parts of the world has stopped, even if it had ever begun. In some ways progress has reversed. Campbell suggests that although the nature of patriarchy appears to have changed, new inequalities are emerging in society. A new era of patriarchy has emerged in which violence has proliferated, self-hatred has flourished and violence against women, especially rape, is committed daily with impunity. Sex trafficking thrives. Campbell calls for a new revolution against this neo-patriarchy.

Patriarchal ideas are entrenched in culture and traditions. In many parts of the world, men continue to presume superiority over women, and gains in equality are either still in their infancy or have not yet left the ground. Certainly, not all women enjoy the same benefits or opportunities. Women in some countries continue to struggle for basic needs and freedoms. Many women struggle to bring up families in poverty and unsanitary conditions and worse. Too many women are under constant threat from sexual predators, who continue to see women merely as sexual objects for their personal gratification. Girls are denied access to education and many are 'married off' as child brides in what is really an institutional form of child abuse. Millions of women are subjected to genital mutilation in the name of 'tradition and culture' and have no access to contraception or to safe abortion. At the same time, many women in the developed world are trapped in a cycle of 'youth and beauty', slaves to advertising and male notions of womanhood.

We have seen examples of how men as a group have controlled women and their bodies; this continues as a major issue, even in countries where women have gained a level of equality. Women's bodies and responsibilities are controlled through the continued belief in patriarchal gender stereotypes, role expectations, marriage and the control of access to family planning, contraception and abortion. Many women have no choice other than to service men both sexually and domestically. Underpinning reasons offered for the continued control of women and their bodies are those of 'tradition' and 'culture'. Mining down into these traditions reveals the true 'reasons' why the control of women and control of their bodies continue; the bedrock of many traditions, religions and cultures is the ideology of patriarchy. Patriarchal notions about male superiority, and the need to control and use women, continue to underpin religious and cultural traditions, even at the beginning of the twenty-first century.

On our trail, we have exposed the foundational myths upon which the ideology of patriarchy depends. The beliefs associated with semen are the 'missing link' in explanations for male superiority. Fantasies surrounding semen are the basis for presumed male superiority, and gender stereotypes of masculinity and femininity. Semen, as the initiator of new life, provided the 'proof' for man as the superior human, and ultimately justified the use and abuse of women. Religious and secular beliefs have supported and sustained these ideas, discourse and practice. During the twentieth century, a plethora of international organisations and institutions tried to address the inequities, discrimination and exclusion of one-half of the human race. Conspicuous by their absence are the leaders of the world's three Abrahamic religions. Religious and cultural traditions require a scrutiny, evaluation and revision of religious 'truths' about male superiority if the scandal of the subjection of one-half of the human race is to be eradicated.

The United Nations (UN) and the World Health Organisation (WHO) in particular have attempted to address the issues. That the United Nations has recognised women's inequality at all is in itself a victory for common sense. It shines a light on women's life experiences, their needs and wants. It recognises the contribution that women make and could make to the world. The UN acknowledges that many women and young girls have little control over their own bodies or over their own lives; and many are subjected to prejudice and discrimination. The WHO examines the consequences for the health of women and girls as a result of these issues. It is through the prism of these organisations that we shall now complete our journey, in order to discover the areas where women's subordination continues.

In 1948, just after the Second World War, many nations came together as the UN. The aim was to see what could be done to prevent the atrocities that some people had inflicted on others during this conflict (based on sexual orientation, political or religious beliefs, ethnicity or way of life) from ever happening again. The delegates discussed the basic 'rights' of the human person based on their humanity alone. The UN agreed an International Bill of Human Rights. The legal document, the Universal Declaration of Human Rights (UDHR)[2] aimed to protect the basic human rights of the individual. The International Bill of Human Rights also included civil, political, economic, social and cultural rights. Over the following decades many countries signed up to the declaration, and some countries have seen improvements in the rights of the citizens. However, the human-rights record in many countries is still a matter for concern. In (mainly) Western countries, women's rights have improved, but there remains some way to go even here. In the developing countries and in those countries that have not committed to basic human rights the subordinate status of women continues as a fact. Contemporary evidence for this can be found in the continued attempts by the UN to improve the lives of women worldwide.

At the end of the twentieth century, it was evident that women continued to be less equal and less powerful than men were. At the turn of the twenty-first century the UN marked the occasion with a list of 'Millennium Goals', because women and girls continue to suffer from discrimination and violence in every part of the world.

Millennium Goal 5, gender equality, focused on women and girls. In the introduction to Goal 5, the overall aim was stated as 'to achieve gender equality and empower all women and girls'.[3] The UN states that gender equality is a fundamental human right. Women and girls should have the same access to education, health care, work and political and economic decision-making processes as men. Women should not be denied access based on sex alone. Interestingly, the UN adds another dimension to women's equality.

> [Gender Equality] is a necessary foundation for a peaceful, prosperous and sustainable world.[4]

In the second decade of the new millennium there is evidence that the battle for women's equality continues; and traditional patriarchal gender stereotypes persist. On 15 January 2015, under Goal 17, the UN hosted the UN 'Barbershop' Conference, which aimed to

> dispel stereotypes, promote gender equality . . . to promote change in how men and boys think and talk about women's empowerment and gender equality.[5]

In March 2015, *the UN set new equality targets for 2030* and member states were told that they must 'step it up' on gender parity; and *the UN labour agency said, 'Women's workplace equality may still take "decades"*. Women earn on average seventy-seven per cent of what men earn.' If things remain the same, 'Equity between women and men will not be achieved before 2086.'[6] In June 2015, the Secretary General of the UN, Ban Ki-moon, said that although there had been successes in the empowerment of women, member states must 'push further' in the struggle to ensure the right to education for all girls. In September 2015, UN Women (the UN entity dedicated to achieving women's empowerment and gender equality) and China co-hosted a gender-equality event at the same time as world leaders met to discuss the issue of sustainable development. Secretary General Ban Ki-moon declared that the new global goals could not be achieved 'without full and equal rights for half of the world's population, in law and in practice'.[7]

There were a few positive moves in 2015 towards women's empowerment and gender equality. In January 2015, at the World Economic Forum in Davos, Switzerland, UN Women enlisted the support of world leaders to end inequalities faced by women and girls worldwide.[8] In July 2015, the UN said that investments which target the development of women and girls around the world are needed to break gender inequality and discrimination.[9] In September 2015, business leaders pledged investments worth millions to boost gender equality.[10] For example, the Bill & Belinda Gates Foundation and Unilever committed millions of dollars to promote gender parity. As regards the representation of women in political decision-making, in 2015, according to the UN, it is noteworthy that it is Africa, not the developed world, that leads in female representation in parliaments. Africa also has one of the highest rates of female entrepreneurship. However, more needs to be done to help Africa's women with a range of other issues, such as domestic and stranger violence, rape, and better access to education, work and health care.

The work of the UN and the WHO is an encouraging beginning on the road to equality for women. However, their efforts are often blocked by appeals to tradition, religion and/or culture. Tradition, religion and culture are interlinked and support patriarchal ideas and stereotypes. The world religions must revise their beliefs about women if basic human rights for all women are to be achieved. Attention must be given to the primary justification for male superiority – the fantasies surrounding semen. Unexposed until now, these fantasies are implicated in violence towards women, control of women's bodies and reproduction, and the objectification of women. It is time for the world's religious leaders to accept the mistakes of the past and apologise to women for their part in the denigration of women.

CHAPTER THIRTEEN:

DIVINE LIQUID TO FERTILISER

In the twenty-first century, violence against women in its many forms continues unabated. Unequal gender relations are entrenched in cultural and social norms. There are no reassessments of age-old myths and resulting stereotypes, roles and responsibilities by any of the main patriarchal religions. The justification for patriarchy, in the public and private spheres, ultimately depends on the fantasies surrounding semen. Once these fantasies are exposed, patriarchal beliefs about male superiority collapse like a house of cards. What is remarkable is that the discovery of the ovum has made little difference to patriarchal attitudes and structures. Either the philosophical and religious justifications for male superiority based in the mythology of semen are not clearly understood, or these mythical origins have become obscured in the mists of time. It is necessary therefore to return to the *roots and justifications* from which presumptions of male superiority arose if patriarchy is to be eradicated.

The UN continues in its attempt to halt the reprehensible levels of violence against women, but cannot succeed alone. Patriarchal institutions of state and religion have a moral responsibility to support the initiatives by the UN and other agencies. In particular, Judaism, Christianity and Islam have an obligation to examine and revise their beliefs in male superiority in the light of new scholarship. For many people what the world religions say has an impact on their lives. The world religions must speak out against violence against women. In particular, they must speak out against rape in all its forms. Rape is one of the most violent forms of sexual abuse against women, men and children. In some countries, legislation continues to allow rapists to escape punishment, and some of these countries are theocracies. The UN survey of July 2013 showed that 424,684 cases of rape and sexual assault were recorded by police in 2011.[1] Non-consensual, forced, sexual experiences and sexual assault are also perpetrated on heterosexual men, homosexual men, boys, adolescent males and even infants. The excuses men give for rape pale into insignificance when small children and infants are the victims. What is evident is that some men cannot control themselves and their lust. In the twenty-first century, rape continues to be used as a tool to suppress and control women.

There is a link between culture and rape. Noteworthy elements of culture are religion, tribal or feudal systems, custom and the judiciary. Unequal gender relations are entrenched in cultural and social norms. In patriarchal societies, these institutions sustain traditional beliefs that support male dominance and the control and objectification of women. The result is sexual discrimination in political, economic and social activities. In traditional patriarchal and fundamentalist religious groups, there is also the issue of blaming the victim and an extreme social stigma is cast on those who have been raped. Rape is also used as a weapon of revenge. Women may be raped in order to 'dishonour' a family when two families are in dispute. 'Tradition' and 'culture' provide 'excuses' for the control and abuse of women in all its forms. Mining down into these traditions reveals that the bedrock of many traditions and cultures is the ideology of patriarchy. Patriarchal notions about male superiority and the need to subordinate women continue to underpin religious and cultural traditions in the twenty-first century.

Patriarchal societies, supported by religion, continue to promote the idea that women and men are 'different' and have different roles and responsibilities in society. Religions and patriarchal organisation have encouraged the presumption that psychosocial gender distinctions are 'natural' and any attempt to alter sex-role assignments is contrary to the natural and divine order. Sex-role assignments are implicated in the control of women and girls, preventable deaths, child marriage, a lack of sex education, few family-planning opportunities, unsafe abortions and so-called 'honour killings'. We have exposed the foundational myths upon which these presumptions rest. Fantasies surrounding semen are the basis of beliefs about a presumed male superiority and gender stereotypes of masculinity and femininity. Semen as the initiator of new life provided the 'proof' for man as the superior human and ultimately justified the use and abuse of women. Religious and secular beliefs supported and sustained the ideas, discourse, sexual stereotypes and practices that continue to provide justification for the use and abuse of women. Therefore religions have a responsibility to reassess sexual stereotypes and doctrines in the light of the downgraded status of semen and its links to a presumed male superiority.

The UN continues in its attempt to improve the lives of women worldwide and to ensure that women access their basic human rights. However, basic human rights (the basic human rights of every individual) are denied to millions of women worldwide. Many women are denied civil, political, economic, social and cultural rights. The human rights record in many countries is still a matter for concern. The fact that some of those countries that deny women their basic human rights are also theocracies highlights the influence of religious ideas on the political and social life. The subordinate status of women continues as a fact of life.

During the twentieth century a plethora of international organisations and institutions have tried to address the inequities, discrimination and exclusion of one-half of the human race. Conspicuous by their continuing appeal to 'differences' and stereotypical roles of women and men are the leaders of the world's three Abrahamic religions, Judaism, Christianity and Islam. Religious and cultural traditions require a scrutiny, evaluation and revision of 'truths' about male superiority if the scandal of the subjection of one-half of the human race is to be eradicated. At the end of the twentieth century, it was evident that women continued to be discriminated against just because they were women.

The UN acknowledges that many women and young girls have little control over their own bodies or over their own lives; and many are subjected to prejudice and discrimination. The WHO examines the consequences for the health of women and girls as a result of these issues. It is through the prism of these organisations that we can see that women's subordination continues. The Millennium Goals aimed to address discrimination and violence against women and girls in every part of the world. Gender equality and empowerment of women is a fundamental human right. Women should not be denied access to education, health care, work or political and economic decision-making processes based on sex alone. Equal rights for half of the world's population, in law and in practice, are an ongoing goal. The battle for women's equality continues and will continue until traditional patriarchal gender stereotypes persist. Persist they will until the fantasies surrounding semen are exposed for the nonsense they are.

It is not enough for international secular organisations such as the WHO and the UN to address issues of inequality without the cooperation of the world's religions. Religious dogma, tradition and culture combine to perpetuate the very inequalities that the secular organisations try to eliminate. As patriarchal religions have played such a significant role in the support and sustenance of the ideology of patriarchy, they should support these initiatives by reviewing and revising doctrines based on beliefs in male superiority. Religious leaders have a primary responsibility to dismantle the beliefs, traditions and structures that support patriarchy and in so doing would help to eradicate much suffering in the world. These notions must be reviewed and updated to reflect advances in science. The literal 'truth' of the Bible must be examined objectively. The three Abrahamic religions continue to accept the 'truth' of the Hebrew Creation stories to support women's inferior status. Woman, cast as the temptress, was the cause of man's sexual arousal. Woman as temptress continues to 'excuse' men for sexual assault and rape. Religious concerns for the protection of semen and its deposit in the 'correct vessel' have also contributed to excuses for rape. Man's 'entitlement' to use women is a principle factor in rape. Religious leaders should acknowledge the contribution of religious ideas as contributory factors in sexual violence against women.

Patriarchal organisations, religions and individual patriarchs continue in their attempt to lock women into 'good' and 'bad' depending on their relationships with men. Women's full potential continues to be lost to humanity. What is needed is a discourse of partnership, of equality between the sexes. The lack of discussion over the discovery of the ovum highlights the continuation of traditional beliefs about male superiority in systems of patriarchy. The presumption of male superiority continues. What this book highlights is the link between a presumed male superiority and semen and the role this has played in secular and religious patriarchy. Discussion will not happen unless the very basis of notions of male superiority is shown to be flawed in its reliance upon the qualities assigned to semen in the ancient world. Semen does not contain the whole foetus in embryo. Semen is not the source of new life: man's role does not elevate him to co-creator with God; man and woman are co-creators of new life. Fantasies about semen continue despite the fact that overnight, semen, the 'divine liquid' of patriarchs, lost its status from the 'seed of new life' to that of a mere fertiliser.

CHAPTER FOURTEEN:

DISCUSSION

The focus of recorded male history has been men and their deeds. It is unsurprising therefore that the period when women assumed a special status due to the ability to produce new life has almost been eradicated from history. The impression is that women have always been weak and dependent on men. Male-centred anthropologists promoted the idea that men were more important to the community because men did the hunting; women's subordinate status was due to the need for protection. However, male domination was not a fact in every society; in some societies, men and women were equal. Our journey to uncover the myths associated with male superiority began in the ancient world, in particular the Greek and Hebrew worlds. As humans attempted to make sense of themselves and the environment, the ideas from Greece together with the Creation stories of the Hebrew Bible were major influences in a patriarchal view of the world. Semen provided the 'proof' for man as the superior being. In the Greek discourse, semen is central to the positive construction of man. Semen is the missing link in theories of male superiority; it provided 'biological evidence' for man's superiority. The possession of semen made man superior to all other forms of life. Semen provided the legitimisation of man's domination of women, children and the natural world. The negative characteristics assigned to woman derived from the lack of semen; physically and mentally weak, she needed man as her guide. The discourse on semen and Hebrew Creation stories provided ongoing legitimacy for patriarchal cultures, norms, traditions, values and religious doctrines.

The possession or lack of semen was instrumental in the patriarchal construction of masculinity and femininity; the control of women and children; and the use and abuse of women as servants and sexual objects. Greek literature (the cultural and philosophical discourses of the Greek, and later Roman, world) provided us with a clear picture of stereotypical notions of 'woman' and 'man', which probably reflected the 'common-sense' notions of the day. In the ancient world one of the things men feared most was that of becoming soft or 'womanish'. The protection of 'vital heat' – that is, semen – became a major preoccupation. Macho man was the order of the day.

Stereotypical images led to specific roles and responsibilities in society. Patriarchal societies, religions and popular attitudes presume that these psychosocial gender distinctions are 'natural' and any attempt to alter sex-role assignments is contrary to the natural and divine order. Patriarchal societies and organisations assign roles to men and women based on these ancient stereotypes. Man, not satisfied with awarding himself the status of the superior sex, also appropriated the primary role in reproduction and elevated himself to 'co-creator' with God. The divine phallus was the source of all that lived. This takeover of birth was a major step in the ultimate total domination of women. Golden balls, orbs, swords and maces adorned monuments as symbols of masculinity and power. Religious justification for male superiority supported the discourse on semen; and a monotheistic male God gradually replaced female gods. In the early orthodox Christian Church, women were assigned the role of 'service', firstly to men and subsequently to the Church. Evidence of women's early participation was removed from sacred texts and women were gradually removed from the public worship. Once orthodox Christianity became the established religion of Imperial Rome, the state became the guarantor of patriarchal power.

The early theologians, especially Augustine, Albert and

Aquinas, provided one of the most significant staging posts on our journey. Augustine linked original sin to sexual intercourse, and identified woman as the site and cause of sin. The focus of Christian sexual theology became genital sex. Albert was confirmed as the patron saint of rapists –'No' cannot be taken seriously as a woman really means yes. Aquinas elevated semen to the 'divine'. The superiority of man and the divinity and protection of semen were cemented into Christian theology, discourse and practice. Over the centuries, the impetus to protect semen intensified. Church celibates intruded into the marital bed, with forbidden times, and 'correct' positions and reasons for the sex act. Contraception was conflated to murder; and the control of women and their bodies intensified.

The Scientific Revolution and the Enlightenment challenged previously held 'truths', and the basis of Christian sexual theology itself. Reason and scientific analysis undermined long-held beliefs and traditions. In the wider world, many traditional lines of authority and institutions were undermined. In the orthodox Church, institutional celibacy remained a bulwark for the fantasies surrounding semen and consequent patriarchal ideas and organisations. The continent male cleric was elevated to an almost angelic state with privileged access to truth. Even in the twenty-first century, celibacy is described as the 'most similar' way of life on earth to a soul in Paradise and therefore the most 'exemplary'. The schism that was the Reformation created the greatest challenge to the power of the celibate clergy. That is, until the twentieth century, when the ban on the birth-control pill led to many Catholics challenging the expertise of the celibates to make decisions about such issues. As a reaction to the Reformation, the Catholic Christian Church reaffirmed orthodox truth as absolute and the Church became a fortress within which priests were 'formed' within a total institution, which had rejected the world. Following the ban on artificial contraception successive popes reaffirmed orthodox traditional teachings as 'truth'. The orthodox Catholic Church continues its patriarchal ideology with its roots in the fantasies surrounding semen. It is a patriarchal Church and the institution of celibacy is an apparatus of power, the backbone of the orthodox Catholic Church.

In the twentieth century, the Second Vatican Council, the 'New Epiphany' for the orthodox Catholic Church, offered no epiphany for semen or for women. John XXIII and Paul VI endorsed the theory of women's equality, but women's role of 'service' continued. There was no revision of traditional theories of male superiority and stereotypical images of woman and of man. The belief that only the male virgin could access truth remained and the traditional power structure itself remained firmly in place. This was despite the loss of papal authority following the encyclical *Humanae Vitae*. Violations against celibacy, which were not dealt with appropriately by successive popes, also resulted in a loss of respect and authority. The attempt to maintain papal power and authority backfired as Catholics effectively removed matters of sexuality to themselves. By the end of the century, the Church was mired in controversies about sexual abuse and the manner in which the Church had dealt with them. Consequently, the power of the Church has dramatically declined in many parts of the world.

In the twentieth and twenty-first centuries, in the wider world, international secular organisations, such as the WHO and the UN, attempted to address issues of inequality, but religious dogma, tradition and culture continue to combine to perpetuate the very inequalities that they try to eliminate. In some parts of the world religion continues to play a major role in politics, culture and the social world. As the three main world religions have played such a significant role in the support and sustenance of the ideology of patriarchy, they have a primary responsibility to dismantle the beliefs, traditions and structures that support patriarchy. The very basis of notions of male superiority rely on semen as the source of new life . . . man as co-creator with God. Despite the fact that the discovery of the ovum demonstrated clearly that semen does not contain the source of new life, but is merely a fertiliser, no religious or secular discussion has linked this discovery to the foundations of patriarchal notions and consequent social and political organisation. Religious leaders should be humble enough to re-examine the basis of their beliefs in male superiority, identify and admit that they got it wrong and accept how those errors have negatively affected women, men and children over the past few thousand years.

They must take an objective look at the stories of Creation. The three Abrahamic religions continue to rely on the literal 'truth' of Hebrew Creation stories to support women's inferior status. Woman, the temptress, was cast as the site and source of sin. Since Adam, man has blamed woman for his sexual arousal. Yet the urge to procreate is necessary for the survival of any species. Arousal is no one's 'fault'. If fault can be applied to sexual arousal, it is what the individual chooses to do with that arousal. If we are to believe the literal truth of the Creation stories Adam chose sexual gratification and thus offended God. Not man enough to take the blame, Adam's excuse of "She tempted me" continues as a defence when many men are charged with rape. Religious admonitions not to spill or waste 'seed' have also provided a sense of entitlement to women's bodies. The WHO states that this sense of entitlement is a principle factor in rape. It also excuses some men in using women merely as receptacles for that 'seed', without regard for the consequences. Stereotypical images of man encourage aggression as a badge of masculinity, which is also a factor in sexual violence towards women.

Individual patriarchs, patriarchal organisations and religions continue in the attempt to control women's bodies and lives. Women's potential has been wasted as socially constructed characteristics assigned to women have focused on women's service to men, children and the sick. Traditional stereotypes have also locked women into 'good' and 'bad' depending on how they provide sexual services to men; motherhood as the main object of life; and woman's presumed all-round incapacity and inferior mental abilities. However, it is more useful to talk about what the human male and female have in common, rather than the duality suggested by traditional stereotypes. This is a crucial discussion to have. All men are not more intelligent than all women; they are not stronger in every way than all women; they are not always the breadwinner; many can control their sexual urges, as can many women; they are not the prime movers in the creation of new life, but are partners with women. In each sex, there are people who carry out the roles and responsibilities traditionally assigned to the other. Acceptance of the notion of partnership is a basis for equality between the sexes. No one sex is superior to the other.

The objectification of women has led to the use and abuse of women. Secular organisations such as the UN and the WHO have recognised that the abuse of women, especially physical violence towards women, continues to be used as a form of control of women; and one of the most effective forms of control in some countries is that of rape. In 2016, the fight to halt violence against women is one of the priorities highlighted by the UN. This attempt by the UN to halt the disgraceful levels of violence against women cannot succeed alone. Patriarchal institutions of state and religion have the greatest impact on the day-to-day lives of people. It is these institutions that require a change in their beliefs about and attitudes towards women.

Religious leaders in particular have a moral responsibility to admit the wrongs perpetuated against women in the name of religion and to redress the balance. In particular, Judaism, Christianity and Islam have a moral obligation to examine and revise their presumptions of male superiority and sexual stereotypes in the light of new scholarship. Failure to do so will demonstrate that the fantasies surrounding semen continue to exist and have meaning. For what the main world religions say affects the everyday lives of tens of millions of people around the world.

REFERENCES

Chapter One: Patriarchy: Men Are Supreme

1. Millett, K., *Sexual Politics*. Andover Press, 1971.
2. Ibid.
3. Stoller, R. J., *Sex and Gender*. Hogarth Press, 1968.
4. Walby, S., *Theorising Patriarchy*. Blackwell, 1994.
5. Janssen-Jurriet, M. L., S*exism: The Male Monopoly on Historical Thought*. Moberg, V. (translator). Farrar Straus, 1982.
6. Anderson, B. A., and Zinsser, J. P., *A History of Their Own: Women in Europe from Prehistory to the Present*, Volumes I and II. Penguin Books, 1990.
7. Pagels, E., *The Gnostic Gospels*. Penguin, 1990.
8. Anderson, B. A., and Zinsser, J. P., *A History of Their Own: Women in Europe from Prehistory to the Present*, Volumes I and II. Penguin Books, 1990.
9. Janssen-Jurriet, M. L., *Sexism: The Male Monopoly on Historical Thought*. Moberg, V. (translator). Farrar Straus, 1982.
10. Anderson, B. A., and Zinsser, J. P., *A History of Their Own: Women in Europe from Prehistory to the Present*, Volumes I and II. Penguin Books, 1990.
11. Ranke-Heinemann, U., *Eunuchs for the Kingdom of Heaven: The Catholic Church and Sexuality*. Heinegg, P. (translator). Penguin, 1991.

Chapter Two: Semen: The Missing Link

Chapter Two is a summary of the Greek discourse on man and woman in the ancient world as outlined in detail in Brown, P., *The Body and Society: Men, Women and Sexual Renunciation in Early Christianity*. Faber & Faber, London, 1991.

1. Shulchan Aruch (Even Ha'ezer, Chapter 23). *http://www. jewishanswers.org/ask-the-rabbi-category/social-issues/ sexuality/?p=498.*
2. Onians, R. B., *The Origins of European Thought*. Cambridge, 1951.
3. Galen, *Galeni Opera Omnia*. Kühn, C. G. (editor). K. Knobloch, 1823. In Kühn, C. G. (editor), 1823, *Galeni Opera, Volume 4: De Semine*. Cited in Brown, 1991.
4. Foucault, M., *The History of Sexuality*, Volume 1. Pelican, 1981.
5. Aristotle, *Physiognomica*. In Forster, R. (editor), *Physiognomici graeci*, Volume 1. Teubner, 1983. Cited in Brown, 1991.
6. Aretaeus, *The Extant Works of Aretaeus the Cappadocian*. Adams, F. (translator). The Sydenham Society, 1856. Cited in Brown, 1991.
7. Galen, *Galeni Opera Omnia*. Kühn C. G. (editor). K. Knobloch, 1823. In Kühn, C. G. (editor), 1823, *Galeni Opera*, Volume 4.
8. *De Semine*. Cited in Brown, 1991.
9. Lefkowitz, M. R., and Fant, M. B., *Women's Life in Greece and Rome*. A source book in translation. Butterworths, 1982.

Chapter Three: Eve the Temptress, Adam the Wimp

1. Trible Phyllis, *Eve and Adam: Genesis 2–3 Reread*. Andover Newton Theological School.

2. Meyers Carol, *Rediscovering Eve: Ancient Israelite Women in Context*. Oxford University Press, 1983.

3. Millett Kate, *Sexual Politics*. Granada Publishing, 1969.

4. Daly, Mary, *Beyond God the Father: Toward a Philosophy of Women's Liberation*. Beacon Press, Boston, 1973.

5. 1 Corinthians 11:7–9

6. Tertullian, 'On the Apparel of Women' in Kvam, Kirsten E., Schearing, Linda S., and Zieglar, Valerie H. (editors), *Eve and Adam: Jewish, Christian and Muslim Reading of Genesis*, pages 132–33. Indiana University Press, 1999.

7. Luther, M., 'Letters on Genesis' in Kvam, Kirsten E., Schearing, Linda S., and Zieglar, Valerie H. (editors), *Eve and Adam: Jewish, Christian and Muslim Reading of Genesis*, pages 267–74. Indiana University Press, 1999.

Chapter Four: Stereotypes As a Weapon

1. Lefkowitz, M. R., and Fant, M. B., *Women's Life in Greece and Rome*. A source book in translation. Butterworths, 1982.

2. Foucault, M., *The History of Sexuality*, Volume 1. Pelican, 1981.

3. Miles, R., *The Women's History of the World*. Paladin, 1989.

4. Galen, *Galeni Opera Omnia*. Kühn, C. G. (editor). K. Knobloch, 1823.

5. Brown, P., *The Body and Society: Men, Women and Sexual Renunciation in Early Christianity*. Faber & Faber, 1991.

6. Foucault, M., *The History of Sexuality*, Volume 1. Pelican, 1981.

7. Lefkowitz, M. R., and Fant, M. B., *Women's Life in Greece and Rome*. A source book in translation. Butterworths, 1982.

8. Lewis, N., and Reinhold, M., *Civilisation, Volume 2: The Roman Empire*. A source book. Harper & Row, 1996.

9. Anderson, B. A., and Zinsser, J. P., *A History of Their Own: Women in Europe from Prehistory to the Present*, Volumes I and II. Penguin Books, 1990.

10. For a discussion on the impact of Greek mythology on traditions which have subordinated women see Anderson and Zinsser, 1990, pages 15–23.

11. Lowe, M., and Hubbard, R. Ruth, *Woman's Nature: Rationalisations of Inequality*. New York & Oxford, 1983.

12. Pagels, E., *The Gnostic Gospels*. Penguin, 1990.

13. Edwardes, A., *The Duel in The Lotus: A Historical Survey of the Sexual Culture of the East*. Edward Arnold, 1965.

14. *The Book of Thomas the Contender*, 144.8-10 in the Nag Hammadi Library (NHL) cited in Pagels, 1990.

15. *The Paraphrase of Shem*, 27.2-6 in NHL: 320 cited in Pagels, 1990.

Chapter Five: The Divine Phallus: The Source of Male Power

1. Gibbon, E., *Historian of the Roman Empire*. Cited in Miles, R., 1989.

2. Miles, R., *The Women's History of the World*. Paladin, 1989.

3. Fraser, James, *The Bough*, 1922; Mead, Margaret, *A study of the Sexes in a Changing World*, 1949; and Hawkes, Jacquetta, *Dawn of the Gods*, 1958, and *Pre-history*, 1965.

4. Evans, Arthur, *The Palace of Minos at Knossos*, Volume 3, 1921–35.

5. Miles, R., *The Women's History of the World*. Paladin, 1989.

6. Ibid.

7. Anderson, B. A., and Zinsser, J. P., *A History of Their Own: Women in Europe from Prehistory to the Present*, Volumes I and II. Penguin Books, 1990.

8. Ibid.

9. Ibid.

10. Ibid.

11. Suttie, Ian D., *The Origins of Love and Hate*, 1960/87.

12. Shuttle, P., and Redgrove, P., *The Wise Wound: Menstruation and Everywoman*. London, 1978/66.

13. Miles, R., *The Women's History of the World*. Paladin, 1989.

14. Ibid.

15. Ibid.

16. Ibid.

17. Anderson, B. A., and Zinsser, J. P., *A History of Their Own: Women in Europe from Prehistory to the Present*, Volumes I and II. Penguin Books, 1990.

18. De Riencourt, A., *Women and Power in History*. London, 1956.

Chapter Six: Women: From Priests to Mere Observers in the Early Christian Church

1. Pagels, E., *The Gnostic Gospels*. Penguin, 1990.

2. Ibid.

3. Ibid.

4. Ibid.

5. Irenaeus, A. H., 1.2.2-3. 5; Irenaeus, 1.4.1-1.5.4. 5

6. Bauer, W., *Orthodoxy and Heresy in Earliest Christianity* (translated from second edition). Philadelphia, 1971.

7. Perkins, P., *The Gnostic Dialogue*. New York, 1979.

8. At 26.20-21 in the Nag Hammadi Library.

9. Pagels, E., *The Gnostic Gospels*. Penguin, 1990.

10. Brown, P., *The Body and Society: Men, Women and Sexual Renunciation in Early Christianity*. Faber & Faber, 1991.

11. Irenaeus, A. H., 1.13.3-4.

12. Ibid.

13. Brown, P., *The Body and Society: Men, Women and Sexual Renunciation in Early Christianity*, page 52. Faber & Faber, 1991.

14. Pagels, E., *The Gnostic Gospels*. Penguin, 1990.

15. Acts of Paul & Thecla 7, New Testament Apocrypha, 2.355.

16. Brown, P., *The Body and Society: Men, Women and Sexual Renunciation in Early Christianity*, page 52. Faber & Faber, 1991.

17. *Tertullian de Praescr* 41. *Tertullian de Baptismo* 1.

18. *Paedagogus*, 111, 79, 4.

19. *Paedagogus*, 11, 33, 2.

20. 'Twenty-Sixth Homily on Cor.', 11:5.

21. Apostolic Constitutions, 1, 9.

22. *Paedagogus*, 111, 50, 1.

23. Brooten, B., *Frauenbefreiung: Biblische and Theologische Argumente*. E. Moltmann-endel, 1978.

24. Kee, A., *The Church of Constantine*. Longman, 1982.

Chapter Seven: Semen and the Foundations of Sexual Theology

1. Sermons, 151:8.

2. *De Bono Con*, 2.

3. *De Genesi ad Litteram*, 9. 5-9.

4. Ranke-Heinemann, U., *Eunuchs for the Kingdom of Heaven: The Catholic Church and Sexuality*. Heinegg, P. (translator). Penguin, 1991.

5. *Tertullian de Exhortatione Castis*, 10.1-2. *Summa Theologiae* 1/i; q 829 4 ad 3.

6. *Confessions*, IX, 9.

7. Augustine, *Against Julian* 1, 48.

8. *Opus Imperfectum* 3.142:1303.

9. *Contra Julianum*, 4, 2, 7:739.

10. *Confessions*, IX, 6.

11. *The City of God*, XIV, 23.

12. *De Doctrine Christiana*, 3, 18.

13. *De Bono Conjugali*, 17, 20.

14. *Against Faustus*, 15, 7.

15. *Questiones Super de Animalibus*, XV q, 11.

16. *Questiones Super de Animalibus*, XII q, 18.

17. Copleston, F. C., *Aquinas*, page 67. Penguin, 1982.

18. *De Animalibus*, 1, 250.

19. *Summa Theologiae*, 1 q, 99 a, 2 ad 2.

20. *Summa Theologiae*, 1 q, 92 q, 1.

21. *De Animalibus*, 1, 25.

22. *De Malo*, 15, 2.

23. *De Bono Con*, 13.

24. Ranke-Heinemann, U., *Eunuchs for the Kingdom of Heaven: The Catholic Church and Sexuality*. Heinegg, P. (translator). Penguin, 1991.

25. *Summa Theologiae*, 11/11 q, 154 a, 11.

26. *Summa Contra Gentiles*, 111, 122.

27. Bernard of Siena (d.1444), quoted in Ranke-Heinemann, 1991.

28. Noonan, J. T., *Contraception*, page 331. Routledge & Kegan Paul, 1965.

29. *Summa Theologiae*, 11/11 q, 70 a, 3.

30. *Summa Contra Gentiles*, 111, 122.
31. Foucault, M., *The Care of the Self.* Pantheon, 1985.
32. Brown, P. R. L., *A History of Private Life, Volume1: From Pagan Rome to Byzantium.* Harvard University Press, 1987.

Chapter Eight: Institutional Celibacy: The Backbone of the Patriarchal Church

1. Rice, D., *Shattered Vows: Exodus from the Priesthood.* Blackstaff, 1991.
2. Schillebeeckx, E., *Celibacy.* Sheed & Ward, 1968.
3. Sipe, A. R. W., *A Secret World: Sexuality and the Search for Celibacy.* Brunner Mazel, 1990.
4. Dolan, J. P., *History of the Reformation.* Desclee & Co, 1965.
5. Kelly, K. T., *New Directions in Moral Theology.* Cassell, 1992.
6. Sipe, A. R. W., *A Secret World: Sexuality and the Search for Celibacy.* Brunner Mazel, 1990.
7. Ibid.

Chapter Nine: The Protestant Reformation; No Reformation for Semen

No references

Chapter Ten: The Twentieth Century: The Protection of Semen Continues

1. Pfliegler, M., *Celibacy.* Sheed & Ward, 1967.

2. Sipe, A. R. W., *A Secret World: Sexuality and the Search for Celibacy*. Brunner Mazel Inc., New York, 1990.

3. Sharp, G., *Patriarchy and Discordant Discourses in the Contemporary Roman Catholic Church*. Unpublished PhD, 1998.

4. Hornsby-Smith, M. P., *Roman Catholic Beliefs in England: Customary Catholicism and Transformations of Religious Authority*. Cambridge University Press, 1996.

5. Hornsby-Smith, M. P., *Roman Catholics in England: Studies in Social Structure Since the Second World War*. Cambridge University Press, 1987.

6. Rice, D., *Shattered Vows: Exodus from the Priesthood*. Blackstaff, 1991.

7. 'Frequently Requested Church Statistics', cara.georgetown. edu., Washington DC Center for Applied Research in the Apostolate. Archived from the original, 20 January 2016; retrieved, 1 February 2016.

8. http://www.catholicherald.co.uk/news/2014/05/05/vatican-statistics-church-growth-remains-steady-worldwide. Accessed, 17 December 2016.

9. 'Message for Vocations Sunday', No. 1193, CTS.

10. Michael O'Loughlin, 'How Did the Church End Up with Married Priests?' *Crux* contributor, 5 August 2014.

11. *The Tablet*, 14 March 1992.

12. Movement for the Ordination of Married Men. Information Bulletin No. 14, 1993.

13. Sipe, A. R. W., *A Secret World: Sexuality and the Search for Celibacy*. Brunner Mazel, 1990.

14. *Sacerdotalis Caelibatus: Encyclical Of Pope Paul VI on the Celibacy of the Priest*, 24 June 1967.

15. Ibid.

16. Ibid.

17. Movement for the Ordination of Married Men, Autumn 1993.

18. Rice, D., *Shattered Vows: Exodus from the Priesthood*. Blackstaff, 1991.
19. *Veritatis Splendor*. CTS, 1993.
20. Rice, D., *Shattered Vows: Exodus from the Priesthood*. Blackstaff, 1991.
21. Sipe, A. R. W., *A Secret World: Sexuality and the Search for Celibacy*. Brunner Mazel, 1990.
22. Sharp, G. See note 3.
23. International Symposium '*Pastores Dabo Vobis*', 28 May 1993.

Chapter Eleven: The Return to Traditional Orthodoxy

1. O' Flannery, Austin, OP (editor), *Humanae Vitae: Vatican Council II: More Post Conciliar Documents*. Fowler Wright Books Ltd, 1982.
2. Yallop, D. A. *In God's Name*. Guild Publishing, 1984.
3. *Casti Connubii*, 31 December 1930. w2.vatican.va/.../ hf_p-xi_enc_19301231_casti-connubii.
4. Sharp, G., *Patriarchy and Discordant Discourses in the Contemporary Roman Catholic Church*. Unpublished PhD, 1998.
5. Ibid.
6. *Gaudium et Spes*, 7 December 1967. www.vatican.va/.../ vat-ii_cons_19651207.
7. *De Sacerdotali Ordinatione Vitis Tantum Reservanda* (On Reserving Priestly Ministry to Men Alone), June 1994.
8. Ibid.
9. Neuner, J., SJ, and Dupuis, J., SJ (editors). *The Christian Faith in the Doctrinal Documents of the Catholic Church*. Collins, 1983.
10. Häring, B., (CSSR), *Healing and Revealing*. St Paul Publications, 1984.

11. Neuner, J., SJ, and Dupuis, J., SJ (editors). See note 9.

12. Häring, B., *Theology of Protest*. Farrar Straus Giroux, 1970.

13. Bianchi, E., and Radford, Ruether R. (editors), *A Democratic Catholic Church: The Reconstruction of Roman Catholicism*. Crossroad, 1992.

14. *Veritatis Splendor (VS): Encyclical Letter Addressed by the Supreme Pontiff Pope John Paul II to All the Bishops of the Catholic Church*. CTS, London, 1993.

15. *L'Osservatore Romano*, 10 October 1983.

16. *Against Faustus*, 15, 7.

17. *Familiaris Consortio*, 22 November 1981. w2.vatican. va/.../hf_jp-ii_exh_19811122_familiaris-consortio.html.

18. *Letter to Women*, 1995. w2.vatican.va/.../john-paul-ii/en/letters/1995/documents/...women.html.

19. Ibid.

20. Theologian Hans Küng on Pope Benedict: 'A Putinization of the Catholic Church'. The German news magazine *Der Spiegel*, 21 September 2011.

21. Clohessy, David, executive director of the Survivors Network of Rape Victims of the Catholic Church. www.rapevictimsofthecatholicchurch.wordpress.com/tag/david.

22. Cassidy, John, 'The Disastrous Influence of Pope Benedict XVI'. *The New Yorker*. www.newyorker.com/news/john-cassidy/...influence-of-pope-benedict-xvi.

23. Butt, Riazat, 'Pope Claims Condoms Could Make African Aids Crisis Worse'. *The Guardian*, 17 March 2009.

24. Wynne-Jones, Jonathan, 'The Pope Drops Catholic Ban on Condoms in Historic Shift'. *The Telegraph*, Monday 11 April 2016.

Chapter Twelve: Patriarchy Disguised As 'Tradition' or 'Culture'

1. Campbell, B., *End of Equality*. Seagull Books, 2013.
2. United Nations. 'The Universal Declaration of Human Rights'. http://www.un.org/en/universal-declaration-human-rights/declaration on human rights.
3. United Nations. 'Millennium Development Goals'. www. un.org/millenniumgoals 2001.
4. United Nations. 'Secretary General Statements'. http:// www.un.org/sustainabledevelopment/gender-equality/.
5. http://www.un.org/sustainabledevelopment/blog/2015/01/ un-barbershop-conference-aims-dispel-stereotypes-promote-gender-equality/.
6. United Nations. 'Sustainable Development: Targets for 2030'. https://sustainabledevelopment.un.org/topics March 2015.
7. 'UN Women at the UN General Assembly / European Year for Development'. europa.eu/eyd2015/en/un-women/ events/un-women-un-general.
8. Global Agenda World Economic Forum Annual Meeting, January 2015, Davos, Switzerland. www3.weforum.org/ docs/AM15.
9. United Nations. 'Secretary General Statements'. www. un.org/sg/statements/index.
10. Global Agenda World Economic Forum Annual Meeting, January 2015, Davos, Switzerland. www3.weforum.org/ docs/AM15.

Chapter Thirteen: Divine Liquid to Fertiliser

1. www.unodc.org/documents/data-and-analysis/statistics/ crime/CTS_Sexual_violence.xls. Accessed, 6 September 2016.

Chapter Fourteen: Discussion

No references

FURTHER READING

Books & Journals

Baigent, M., and Leigh, R., *The Dead Sea Scrolls Deception.* Jonathon Cape, 1992.

Daly, K., and Bouhours, B., 'Rape and Attrition in the Legal Process: A Comparative Analysis of Five Countries', *Crime and Criminal Justice: A Review of Research*, Volume 39, pages 565–650.

De Sacerdotalis Ordinatione Viris Tantum Reservanda, 1994. w2.vatican.va/.../hf_jp-ii_apl_19940522_ordinatio-sacerdotalis.html.

Gaudium et Spes, 7 December 1967. www.vatican.va/.../vat-ii_cons_19651207.

'Holy Father Condemns Contraception in Strongest Terms', quoted in *The Wanderer*, 29 September 1983.

Kalbfleisch, P. J., and Cody, M. J., *Gender Power and Communication in Human Relationships.* Routledge, 2012. ISBN 1-136-48050-1.5.

Kelly, G., 'UCSB's SexInfo'. Soc.ucsb.edu. Retrieved, 31 December 2010. *Sexuality Today*, tenth edition. McGraw-Hill, New York, 2011. ISBN 978-0-07-353199-1.

Mcclory, Robert, *Turning Point: The Inside Story of the Papal Birth Control Commission, and How Humanae Vitae*

Changed the Life of Patty Crowley and the Future of the Church. Crossroad, New York, 1995.

Niebuhr, G., 'Broken Vows: When Priests Take Lovers', *The Atlanta Journal*, 15 April 1989.

Pontifical council for the family. *Vademecum for Confessors Concerning Some Aspects of the Morality of Conjugal Life*, 1997.

Ranke-Heinemann, U., *Eunuchs for the Kingdom of Heaven: The Catholic Church and Sexuality*. Heinegg, P. (translator). Penguin, 1991.

Shannon, William Henry, *The Papal Commission on Birth Control: The Lively Debate: Response to Humanae Vitae*, pages 76–104. Sheed & Ward, New York, 1970.

Veritatis Splendor, 1993.

Other Publications

Human Rights Watch. *Q & A: Child Marriage and Violations of Girls' Rights*.

Shaqaeq Arab Forum for Human Rights. 'Say What? Say What?' blogs.app.com/saywhat/tag/shaqaeq-arab-forum-for-human-rights.

'UN Secretary General Announces $25 Billion in Initial Commitments to End Preventable Deaths of Women, Children and Adolescents by 2030', 26 September 2015.

UNFPA ESARO. 'Gender-Based Violence'. http://www.unfpa.org/gender-based-violence.

United Nations.
   VAW – 'Indicators on Violence Against Women'. www.un.org/womenwatch/daw/vaw/v-issues-focus.htm. A/RES/48/104. 'Declaration on the Elimination of Violence' Secretary General Ban Ki-Moon's Statements, 2015. www.un.org/sg/statements.

Secretary General Ban Ki-Moon's Statements, 2016. www.un.org/sg/statements.

Sustainable Development Goals, March 2015. www.un.org/sustainabledevelopment/blog/2015/03/member-states-must.

'The Eighth United Nations Survey on Crime Trends and the Operations of Criminal Justice Systems', 2001–02 – Table 02.08: Total recorded rapes. unodc.org.

'UN Action Against Sexual Violence in Conflict'. www.stoprapenow.org2.

WHO. Sixty-First World Health Assembly, Geneva, 19–24 May 2008. www.who.int.